SMALL *Oxford* BOOKS

THE TRAIN

SMALL *Oxford* BOOKS

THE TRAIN

Compiled by
ROGER GREEN

Oxford New York Toronto Melbourne
OXFORD UNIVERSITY PRESS
1982

Oxford University Press, Walton Street, Oxford OX2 6DP

London Glasgow New York Toronto
Delhi Bombay Calcutta Madras Karachi
Kuala Lumpur Singapore Hong Kong Tokyo
Nairobi Dar es Salaam Cape Town
Melbourne Auckland

and associates in
Beirut Berlin Ibadan Mexico City Nicosia

British Library Cataloguing in Publication Data
The Train. — (Small Oxford books)
1. Railroads — Trains — Literary collections
I. Green, Roger
820.8'0356   PR1111.T/
ISBN 0–19–214127–9

Library of Congress Cataloging in Publication Data
Main entry under title:
The Train. — (Small Oxford books)   Includes index
1. Railroad travel—Literary collections
2. English literature.   I. Green, Roger
RR1111.R35T7   820'.8'0356   81–16947
ISBN 0–19–214127–9   AACR2

*

To the memory of
HUGO DYSON
who loved trains
and never missed
a connection

Set by Western Printing Services Ltd.
Printed in Great Britain by
Hazell Watson & Viney Limited
Aylesbury, Bucks

Introduction

This anthology is about trains. It is about *the* train – an idea as well as a reality. It begins at the beginning, and ends at what I see as very nearly the end. It is not a history, although a fair amount of history emerges from it. It is not an exhaustive survey, but a brief excursion with British and American writers as conductors.

If I am to declare my interest, then I must admit that I am a commuter, certainly not a railway buff. When I think of 'the train', what first comes to mind is always that conveyance, which I love and hate, which carries me to and from London every day. However, the further I proceeded with the work of compilation, the more I became aware of the unique aura and attributes of 'the train' in its broadest sense. I hope that readers of this anthology will come away with their awareness similarly heightened.

The train is its own world. It is literally a place apart. It is on the land and yet not of it. There is nothing like it. The mystique of ships is quite different. Airliners have no mystique. Motor cars are mere mobile boxes. But the train – linked rolling-stock of every description, drawn along iron rails by a locomotive, able to convey anything and anyone almost anywhere in the world – what an extraordinary idea!

When the train carries passengers, it carries them *doing things*: eating, sleeping, reading, writing, thinking, gazing, talking, walking, standing, sitting, lying down, making love, murdering, dying; practising these and many other pursuits while passing through, by day or at night, industrial cities or deserted landscapes with which they have no connection whatsoever. You can drink hot tea from a samovar in a warm compartment in freezing Siberia. You can watch people and animals wilting in the boiling sun from the cool comfort of an air-conditioned train in India. Commonplace actions are put in a new perspective. Incongruity is the keynote.

The train seems to have such character. Yet, as several of the writers in the following pages stress, the train is totally passive, impartial, inanimate. It is more neutral than the jungle, and just as full of the strange and the unexpected. All mystery – or ordinariness, for that matter – that the train appears to have is imposed upon it by us. 'Romance brought up the nine-fifteen', wrote Rudyard Kipling. It is a line that, for some reason, has caught people's imaginations; but it means no more than that, if you look for it, you can find romance anywhere, though perhaps you stand a better chance on the nine-fifteen than on the eight-fifteen crowded with commuters.

So that is partly what this anthology deals with: how a prosaic and logical invention has worked its way into the hearts and minds of men, over one and a half centuries, to re-emerge in all kinds of manifestations, some not logical or prosaic at all. It also deals with the journey, but only incidentally. When we travel by car or by bus, for instance, we usually ignore the vehicle. But when we travel by train, whether to Paddington or Patagonia, the train itself provides a major part of the experience. The anthology concentrates on the train's contribution.

The selection of extracts has been entirely governed by what I either already knew or else turned up in the course of rather haphazard research. Some omissions are due to ignorance, others to lack of space, and still others to my failure to track them down. In the last category comes the Duke of Wellington's alleged disapproval of railways 'because they will encourage the lower classes to move about'; I could not find chapter and verse for this and, indeed, turned up some speeches by the Iron Duke very much in favour of the iron horse. Similarly, to my chagrin, I could not discover a quotable version of the tale of poor Branwell Brontë, brother of Anne, Charlotte, and Emily, being sacked, because of drunkenness, from his job as a clerk at Luddendon Foot Station on the Liverpool and Manchester Railway.

The anthology demonstrates, I think, how difficult it is to write badly about trains. As one would expect, when a great writer finds it necessary to describe a locomotive or use a railway metaphor, he does so with all his usual aplomb and panache. As one might not expect, when lesser writers deal with trains, inspired by the subject they rise to new heights.

Another curious fact to emerge is that, if a writer mentions trains at all, he tends to mention them, like the young lady of Spain who was sick in one, again and again and again. I never realized until I began to compile this anthology what prolific alluders to trains are, among others, Walt Whitman, Arnold Bennett, D. H. Lawrence, John Davidson, Louis MacNeice, T. S. Eliot, Dannie Abse, and Ian Fleming. On the other hand, strangely enough, Sir John Betjeman has fewer railway references than one might have expected.

Lastly, the anthology does nothing to resolve, but much to accentuate, the great antithesis, the remarkable paradox of the train. I mean how the train can appear as a hero and as a villain. How it can represent progress and beauty on the one hand, and the rape of landscape and shattering of silence on the other. How it can and does stand with equal validity for two completely opposed sets of ideas: commuting, monotony, routine, squalor, death; travelling, variety, adventure, glamour, life. The fascination and entertainment to be derived from such a rich and potent symbol are – as every schoolboy and many a clergyman know – inexhaustible.

Wolvercote
March 1981

The Beginnings &
Early Reactions

Suddenly the train was here. One minute man could travel no faster on land than a good horse could carry him, the next – by about 1840 – he could avail himself of a network of railways. This enormous change took a lot of adjusting to. The train was not a development of something that had previously existed. It was totally, bewilderingly new. It produced strange noises, smells, dirt. It moved at amazing speeds. It demonstrated remarkable engineering skills. Visually, its like had never been seen before.

Many writers quickly perceived and started to deal with some of the broader issues raised by the existence of railways. But only one seems to have understood immediately all the implications – Charles Dickens. Not only does he give us an accurate analysis, but he is also virtually the only writer to capture the complete novelty and sheer excitement of the first railways. Miraculously, he achieves this merely through a few incidental touches in the course of a long novel, Dombey and Son.

The first shock of a great earthquake had, just at that period, rent the whole neighbourhood to its centre. Traces of its course were visible on every side. Houses were knocked down; streets broken through and stopped; deep pits and trenches dug in the ground; enormous heaps of earth and clay thrown up; buildings that were undermined and shaking, propped by great beams of wood. Here, a chaos of carts, overthrown and jumbled together, lay topsy-turvy at the bottom of a steep unnatural hill; there, confused treasures of iron soaked and rusted in something that had accidentally become a pond. Everywhere were bridges that led nowhere; thoroughfares that were wholly impassable; Babel towers of chimneys, wanting half their height; temporary wooden houses and enclosures, in the most unlikely situations; carcases of ragged tenements, and fragments of unfinished walls and arches, and piles of scaffolding, and wildernesses of bricks, and giant forms of cranes, and tripods straddling above nothing. There were a hundred thousand shapes and substances of incompleteness, wildly mingled out of their places, upside down, burrowing in the earth, aspiring in the air, mouldering in the water, and unintelligible as any dream. Hot springs and fiery eruptions, the usual attendants upon earthquakes, lent their contributions of confusion to the scene. Boiling water hissed and heaved within dilapidated walls; whence, also, the glare and roar of flames came issuing forth; and mounds of ashes blocked up rights of way, and wholly changed the law and custom of the neighbourhood.

In short, the yet unfinished and unopened Railroad was in progress; and, from the very core of all this dire disorder, trailed smoothly away, upon its mighty course of civilisation and improvement.

Dombey and Son began to appear in 1846, not twenty *years since the opening of the first railway. Charles Dickens, as we shall see again in other extracts, had got his ideas sorted out. His contemporary, William Words-worth, was in more of a muddle. In 1833 he came down on the side of progress in this sonnet:*

STEAMBOATS, VIADUCTS, AND RAILWAYS

Motions and Means, on land and sea at war
With old poetic feeling, not for this,
Shall ye, by Poets even, be judged amiss!
Nor shall your presence, howsoe'er it mar
The loveliness of Nature, prove a bar
To the Mind's gaining that prophetic sense
Of future change, that point of vision, whence
May be discovered what in soul ye are.
In spite of all that beauty may disown
In your harsh features, Nature doth embrace
Her lawful offspring in Man's art; and Time,
Pleased with your triumphs o'er his brother Space,
Accepts from your bold hands the proffered crown
Of hope, and smiles on you with cheer sublime.

But by 1844 he had committed a complete volte-face – and written a better sonnet – when a railway threatened to disturb his own peaceful corner of the Lake District.

ON THE PROJECTED KENDAL AND WINDERMERE
RAILWAY, 1844

Is then no nook of English ground secure
From rash assault? Schemes of retirement sown
In youth, and 'mid the busy world kept pure
As when their earliest flowers of hope were blown,
Must perish; – how can they this blight endure?
And must he too the ruthless change bemoan
Who scorns a false utilitarian lure
'Mid his paternal fields at random thrown?

Baffle the threat, bright Scene, from Orrest-head
Given to the pausing traveller's rapturous glance:
Plead for thy peace, thou beautiful romance
Of nature; and, if human hearts be dead,
Speak, passing winds; ye torrents, with your strong
And constant voice, protest against the wrong.

*Towards the end of the century, J. K. Stephen pokes
gentle fun at Wordsworth's vacillation.*

POETIC LAMENTATION ON THE INSUFFICIENCY OF STEAM LOCOMOTION IN THE LAKE DISTRICT

Bright Summer spreads his various hue
    O'er nestling vales and mountains steep,
Glad birds are singing in the blue,
    In joyous chorus bleat the sheep.
But men are walking to and fro,
    Are riding, driving far and near,
And nobody as yet can go
    By train to Buttermere.

The sunny lake, the mountain track,
    The leafy groves are little gain,
While Rydal's pleasant pathways lack
    The rattle of the passing train.
But oh! what poet would not sing
    That heaven-kissing rocky cone,
On whose steep side the railway king
    Shall set his smoky throne?

Helvellyn in those happy days
    With tunnelled base and grimy peak
Will mark the lamp's approaching rays,
    Will hear the whistle's warning shriek:
Will note the coming of the mails,
    And watch with unremitting stare
The dusky grove of iron rails
    Which leads to Euston-square.

Wake, England, wake! 'tis now the hour
  To sweep away this black disgrace –
The want of locomotive power
  In so enjoyable a place.
Nature has done her part, and why
  Is mightier man in his to fail?
I want to hear the porters cry,
  'Change here for Ennerdale!'

Man! nature must be sought and found
  In lonely pools, on verdant banks;
Go, fight her on her chosen ground,
  Turn shapely Thirlmere into tanks:
Pursue her to her last retreats,
  And if perchance a garden plot
Is found among the London streets,
  Smoke, steam and spare it not.

Presumptuous nature! do not rate
  Unduly high thy humble lot,
Nor vainly strive to emulate
  The fame of Stephenson and Watt.
The beauties which thy lavish pride
  Has scattered through the smiling land
Are little worth till sanctified
  By man's completing hand.

J. K. Stephen, *Lapsus Calami*, 1891

Ebenezer Elliott, a Sheffield iron-founder as well as a poet, had a vision of improved communications leading to the abolition of tyranny and better understanding between nations and individuals. He astutely perceived the potential of mechanical means of transport, such as railways, for conveying not only people and goods but also ideas.

They come! the shrieking steam ascends,
  Slow moves the banner'd train;
They rush! the towering vapour bends –
  The kindled wave again
Screams over thousands, thronging all
To witness now the funeral
  Of law-created pain.

For Mind shall conquer time and space;
  Bid East and West shake hands!
Bring, over Ocean, face to face,
  Earth's ocean-sever'd strands;
And, on his path of iron, bear
Words that shall wither, in despair,
  The tyrants of all lands.

From *Verses on the Opening of the
Sheffield and Rotherham Railway*, 1840

*We are brought back to earth by that great pricker of
bubbles, the witty canon of St Paul's, Sydney Smith. He
saw, as early as 1842, that just because it is possible to
pass quickly from A to B, it is not necessarily desirable to
do so. (A 'Solan goose' is another name for a gannet.)*

Railroad travelling is a delightful improvement of
human life. Man is become a bird; he can fly longer
and quicker than a Solan goose. The mamma rushes
sixty miles in two hours to the aching finger of her
conjugating and declining grammar boy. The early
Scotchman scratches himself in the morning mists of
the North, and has his porridge in Piccadilly before the
setting sun. The Puseyite priest, after a rush of 100
miles, appears with his little volume of nonsense at the
breakfast of his bookseller. Everything is near, everything is immediate – time, distance, and delay are
abolished.

Letter to the Editor of the *Morning
Chronicle*, 7 June 1842

In this little charade from Thomas Love Peacock's novel
Gryll Grange (*1860*), *the character Gryllus is supposed to
have just awoken from a sleep of 3,000 years. Naturally
he has to have the modern world, including trains,
explained to him. Like Sydney Smith, Peacock hints that
movement for movement's sake can be a rather futile
activity.*

GRYLLUS.   Now the whole scene is changed.
  I see long chains of strange machines on wheels,
  With one in front of each, puffing white smoke
  From a black hollow column. Fast and far
  They speed, like yellow leaves before the gale,
  When Autumn winds are strongest. Through their
    windows
  I judge them thronged with people; but distinctly
  Their speed forbids my seeing.

SPIRIT-RAPPER.   This is one
  Of the great glories of our modern time,
  'Men are become as birds', and skim like swallows
  The surface of the world.

GRYLLUS.   For what good end?

SPIRIT-RAPPER.
  The end is in itself – the end of skimming
  The surface of the world.

GRYLLUS.   If that be all,
  I had rather sit in peace in my old home:
  But while I look, two of them meet and clash,
  And pile their way with ruin. One is rolled
  Down a steep bank; one through a broken bridge
  Is dashed into a flood. Dead, dying, wounded,
  Are there as in a battlefield. Are these
  Your modern triumphs? Jove preserve me from
    them.

[7]

SPIRIT-RAPPER.

These ills are rare. Millions are borne in safety
Where one incurs mischance.

§

It is ironic that Ruskin cites the Vale of Tempe in Central
Greece as a divine spot unexploited by speculators. Today
a railroad has been 'enterprised' along the entire length of
the sacred gorge. At one point it passes so close to a shrine
that engine-drivers can – and do – toss out their loose
drachmas in an act of propitiation.

There was a rocky valley between Buxton and Bakewell,
once upon a time, divine as the Vale of Tempe; you
might have seen the Gods there morning and evening –
Apollo and all the sweet Muses of the Light – walking
in fair procession on the lawns of it, and to and fro
among the pinnacles of its crags. You cared neither for
Gods nor grass, but for cash (which you did not know
the way to get); you thought you could get it by what
the *Times* calls 'Railroad Enterprise'. You Enterprised
a Railroad through the valley – you blasted its rocks
away, heaped thousands of tons of shale into its lovely
stream. The valley is gone, and the gods with it; and
now, every fool in Buxton can be at Bakewell in half an
hour, and every fool in Bakewell at Buxton; which you
think a lucrative process of exchange – you Fools
Everywhere.

> John Ruskin, *Fors Clavigera, Letters to the*
> *Workmen and Labourers of Great Britain. Letter V*, 1871

Ruskin disliked stations as much as he disliked railways. It was some fifty years or so before G. K. Chesterton came along to put him in his place.

Another of the strange and evil tendencies of the present day is to the decoration of the railroad station. Now, if there be any place in the world in which people are deprived of that portion of temper and discretion which is necessary to the contemplation of beauty, it is there. It is the very temple of discomfort, and the only charity that the builder can extend to us is to show us, plainly as may be, how soonest to escape from it.

The whole system of railroad travelling is addressed to people who, being in a hurry, are therefore, for the time being, miserable. No one would travel in that manner who could help it – who had time to go leisurely over hills and between hedges, instead of through tunnels and between banks: at least, those who would have no sense of beauty so acute as that we need consult it at the station.

The railroad is in all its relations a matter of earnest business, to be got through as soon as possible. It transmutes a man from a traveller into a living parcel. For the time he has parted with the nobler characteristics of his humanity for the sake of a planetary power of locomotion. Do not ask him to admire anything. You might as well ask the wind.

John Ruskin, *The Seven Lamps of Architecture,*
iv. 21, 1849

A railway station is an admirable place, although Ruskin did not think so. He did not think so because he himself was even more modern than the railway station. He did not think so because he was himself feverish, irritable, and snorting like an engine. He could not value the ancient silence of the railway station.

'In a railway station,' he said, 'you are in a hurry, and therefore miserable'; but you need not be either unless you are as modern as Ruskin. The true philosopher does not think of coming just in time for his train except as a bet or a joke.

The only way of catching a train I have ever discovered is to miss the train before. Do this, and you will find in a railway station much of the quietude and consolation of a cathedral. It has many of the characteristics of a great ecclesiastical building; it has vast arches, void spaces, coloured lights, and, above all, it has recurrence or ritual. It is dedicated to the celebration of water and fire, the two prime elements of all human ceremonial. Lastly, a station resembles the old religions rather than the new religions in this point, that people go to it.

G. K. Chesterton, 'The Prehistoric Railway Station',
in *Tremendous Trifles*

§

Meanwhile, across the Atlantic, railways were proliferating and American writers too were working out their attitudes and taking up their positions. The philosopher, poet, and essayist Ralph Waldo Emerson was in no doubt that the train was a Good Thing and that ugliness was in the eye of the beholder.

For, as it is dislocation and detachment from the life of God that makes things ugly, the poet, who re-attaches things to nature and the Whole – re-attaching even artificial things, and violations of nature, by a deeper insight – disposes very easily of the most disagreeable facts. Readers of poetry see the factory-village and the railway, and fancy that the poetry of the landscape is broken up by these; for these works of art are not yet consecrated in their reading; but the poet sees them fall within the great Order not less than the bee-hive or the spider's geometrical web. Nature adopts them very fast into her vital circles, and the gliding train of cars she loves like her own.

'The Poet', from *Essays*, 1841, 1844

Henry David Thoreau, on the other hand, was not so sure, despite being a friend and admirer of Emerson. He wrote in Walden *(1854) about how he spent two years in a cabin in the woods in an attempt to turn his back on modern, increasingly urban, life.*

Men have an indistinct notion that if they keep up this activity of joint stocks and spades long enough all will at length ride somewhere, in next to no time, and for nothing; but though a crowd rushes to the depot, and the conductor shouts 'All aboard!' when the smoke is blown away and the vapour condensed, it will be perceived that a few are riding, but the rest are run over, – and it will be called, and will be, 'A melancholy accident'. No doubt they can ride at last who shall have earned their fare, that is, if they survive so long, but they will probably have lost their elasticity and desire to travel by that time.

This spending of the best part of one's life earning money in order to enjoy a questionable liberty during the least valuable part of it, reminds me of the Englishman who went to India to make a fortune first, in order that he might return to England and live the life of a poet. He should have gone up garret at once. 'What!' exclaim a million Irishmen, starting up from all the shanties in the land, 'is not this railroad which we have built a good thing?' Yes, I answer, *comparatively* good – that is, you might have done worse; but I wish, as you are brothers of mine, that you could have spent your time better than digging in this dirt.

Another American, Nathaniel Hawthorne, produced in
The Celestial Railroad *a rare example of an allegorical
treatment of the train. Through parody of Bunyan's*
Pilgrim's Progress, *Hawthorne makes the point that
that work is as relevant now (1843) as it ever was, and he
contrives to imply that the so-called progress demonstrated
by the new railways is not as wonderful as its supporters
claim.*

The passengers being all comfortably seated, we now
rattled away merrily, accomplishing a greater distance
in ten minutes than Christian probably trudged over in
a day. It was laughable, while we glanced along, as it
were, at the tail of a thunderbolt, to observe two dusty
foot travellers in the old pilgrim guise, with cockle
shell and staff, their mystic rolls of parchment in their
hands and their intolerable burdens on their backs. . .
We greeted the two pilgrims with many pleasant gibes
and a roar of laughter; whereupon they gazed at us with
such woeful and absurdly compassionate visages that
our merriment grew tenfold more obstreperous.
Apollyon also entered heartily into the fun, and
contrived to flirt the smoke and flame of the engine, or
of his own breath, into their faces, and envelop them in
an atmosphere of scalding steam.

*Robert Louis Stevenson travelled by train across central
America in 1879. If only he had not died at the age of
forty-four, he himself might have become the Homer of
'the bad medicine waggon'. As it is we are still waiting.*

Only down the long, sterile cañons, the train shot
hooting and awoke the resting echo. That train was the
one piece of life in all the deadly land; it was the one
actor, the one spectacle fit to be observed in this
paralysis of man and nature. And when I think how
the railroad has been pushed through this unwatered

wilderness and haunt of savage tribes, and now will bear an emigrant for some £12 from the Atlantic to the Golden Gates; how at each stage of the construction, roaring, impromptu cities, full of gold and lust and death, sprang up and then died away again, and are now but wayside stations in the desert; how in these uncouth places pig-tailed Chinese pirates worked side by side with border ruffians and broken men from Europe, talking together in a mixed dialect, mostly oaths, gambling, drinking, quarrelling and murdering like wolves; how the plumed hereditary lord of all America heard, in this last fastness, the scream of the 'bad medicine waggon' charioting his foes; and then when I go on to remember that all this epical turmoil was conducted by gentlemen in frock coats, and with a view to nothing more extraordinary than a fortune and a subsequent visit to Paris, it seems to me, I own, as if this railway were the one typical achievement of the age in which we live, as if it brought together into one plot all the ends of the world and all the degrees of social rank, and offered to some great writer the busiest, the most extended, and the most varied subject for an enduring literary work. If it be romance, if it be contrast, if it be heroism that we require, what was Troy town to this? But, alas! it is not these things that are necessary – it is only Homer.

Robert Louis Stevenson, *Across the Plains*, 1892

So we leave this section, as we began it, with Dickens. He showed us the railway in the making. Now he shows us the railway established and flourishing.

As to the neighbourhood which had hesitated to acknowledge the railroad in its straggling days, that had grown wise and penitent, as any Christian might in such a case, and now boasted of its powerful and prosperous relation. There were railway patterns in its drapers' shops, and railway journals in the windows of its newsmen. There were railway hotels, office-houses, lodging-houses, boarding-houses; railway plans, maps, views, wrappers, bottles, sandwich-boxes, and time-tables; railway hackney-coach and cabstands; railway omnibuses, railway streets and buildings, railway hangers-on and parasites, and flatterers out of all calculation. There was even railway time observed in clocks, as if the sun itself had given in. Among the vanquished was the master chimney-sweeper . . . who now lived in a stuccoed house three stories high, and gave himself out, with golden flourishes upon a varnished board, as contractor for the cleansing of railway chimneys by machinery.

To and from the heart of this great change, all day and night, throbbing currents rushed and returned incessantly like its life's blood. Crowds of people and mountains of goods, departing and arriving scores upon scores of times in every four-and-twenty hours, produced a fermentation in the place that was always in action. The very houses seemed disposed to pack up and take trips. Wonderful Members of Parliament, who, little more than twenty years before, had made themselves merry with the wild railroad theories of engineers, and given them the liveliest rubs in cross-examination, went down into the north with their watches in their hands, and sent on messages before by the electric telegraph, to say that they were coming. Night and day the conquering engines rumbled at their distant work, or, advancing smoothly to their journey's end, and gliding like tame dragons into the allotted corners grooved out to the inch for their reception, stood bubbling and trembling there, making the walls quake, as if they were dilating with the secret knowledge of great powers yet unsuspected in them, and strong purposes not yet achieved.

Dombey and Son, 1846–8

The Train

Once the tracks had been laid, locomotives and rolling-stock multiplied in a marvellous variety of shapes, colours, and functions. Emerson was right – poets, and others, saw them 'fall within the great Order' and began to write about them, not always with starry eyes. The writers also saw the possibilities of the first really new metaphor (in modern Greek metaphora *means both 'metaphor' and 'transport') for hundreds of years.*

A locomotive is, next to a marine engine, the most sensitive thing man ever made.

Rudyard Kipling, '·007' from *The Day's Work*, 1898

It is hard for us to remember that, for some seventy years, the train had the stage to itself as a mechanical means of land transport. There was nothing to relate it to except what had preceded it – the horse. This is what Emily Dickinson does while still conveying the impression that it is a very extraordinary horse indeed with a touch of the supernatural.

I LIKE TO SEE IT LAP THE MILES

> I like to see it lap the Miles –
> And lick the Valleys up –
> And stop to feed itself at Tanks –
> And then – prodigious step
>
> Around a Pile of Mountains –
> And supercilious peer
> In Shanties – by the sides of Roads –
> And then a Quarry pare

THE TRAIN

To fit it's sides
And crawl between
Complaining all the while
In horrid-hooting stanza –
Then chase itself down Hill –

And neigh like Boanerges –
Then – prompter than a Star
Stop – docile and omnipotent
At it's own stable door –

Emily Dickinson (1830–86)

*Even a supernatural horse is too tame for Mary Coleridge.
Her 'wild thing' is almost apocalyptic, and her conclusion
is positively (or maybe one should say 'relatively')
Einsteinian.*

THE TRAIN

A green eye – and a red – in the dark.
Thunder – smoke – and a spark.

It is there – it is here – flashed by.
Whither will the wild thing fly?

It is rushing, tearing thro' the night,
Rending her gloom in its flight.

It shatters her silence with shrieks.
What is it the wild thing seeks?

Alas! for it hurries away
Them that are fain to stay.

Hurrah! for it carries home
Lovers and friends that roam.

Where are you, Time and Space?
The world is a little place,

Your reign is over and done,
You are one.

Mary Coleridge (1861–1907)

It is interesting to note from this description by Surtees that the concept of taking one's vehicle on a train is no new one, but was introduced almost as soon as the railways started. Indeed, in the 1840s, you could even travel in your carriage on a special 'open platform'.

Precisely at three-quarters of a minute before three, a wild shrill whistle, that seemed to issue from the bowels of the earth and turn right up into mid-air, was heard at the back of Shavington Hill, and, in an instant, the engine and long train rounded the base, the engine smoking and snorting like an exasperated crocodile. Nearer and nearer it comes, with a thundering sort of hum that sounds throughout the country. The wondering ploughman stops his team. The cows and sheep stand staring with astonishment, while the horses take a look, and then gallop about the fields, kicking up their heels and snorting with delight. The guard's red coat on the engine is visible – next his gold hat band appears – now we read the Hercules on the engine, and anon it pulls up with a whiff, a puff, and a whistle, under the slate-covered shed, to give the Hercules his water, and set down and take up passengers and goods. Seven first-class passenger carriages follow the engine, all smart, clean, and yellow, with appropriate names on each door panel – The Prince Albert, Queen Victoria, and the Prince of Wales, The Venus, The Mercury, The Comet, and The Star; next come ten second-class ones, green, with covered tops, and half-covered sides, but in neither set is there anything at all like the Jorrocks' party. Cattle-pens follow, holding sheep, swine, donkeys, and poultry; then came an open platform with a broken britzka, followed by a curious-looking nondescript one-horse vehicle, containing a fat man in a low-crowned hat, and a versatio or reversible coat, with the preferable side outwards. Along with him were two ladies muffled up in cloaks, and at the back was a good-looking servant-maid. From the bottom of the carriage swung a couple of hams, and a large warming-pan.

R. S. Surtees, *Handley Cross*, 1843

The strange, rather morbid Scottish poet John Davidson introduces trains into many of his poems, usually with sinister or at least melancholy undertones. But in talking of 'apathetic fatalism', is he really saying any more than that a machine like a train is a totally passive object which can serve any purpose we like to put it to?

> . . . the morning train drew out.
> Leaping along the land from town to town,
> Its iron lungs respired its breath of steam,
> Its resonant flanges, and its vertebral
> Loose-jointed carcase of a centipede
> Gigantic, hugged and ground the parallel
> Adjusted metals of its destined way
> With apathetic fatalism, the mark
> Of all machinery.

John Davidson (1857–1909), *Rail and Road*

§

Charles Causley gives us a glimpse of one pleasant purpose for which trains can be used – or could. Today the train, which seemed to some Victorians to have conquered time and space, has been superseded by the aeroplane which can turn the seasons upside down by wafting daffodils from the Channel Islands, potatoes from Cyprus, or strawberries from California.

There came on the west wind from Scilly
   The iron music of the London train
Carrying its cargo of freshly cut flowers
   To the porters and piazzas of Covent Garden.

From 'At Porth Veor'

Amazingly, in this egalitarian age, class distinction is still practised on the trains, though at least everybody is now protected from the weather. The sole criterion is how much you are prepared to pay for your ticket. British Rail sometimes allows poorer passengers to travel in the rolling-stock normally used by wealthier people. For this contingency they have a very tactfully worded label which refers not to 'Second Class Passengers' but to 'Passengers Travelling Second Class'. However, they usually remove the antimacassars.

§

The rich man has a carriage
   Where no rude eye can flout him;
     The poor man's bane
     Is a third-class train,
With the daylight all about him.

Thomas Love Peacock (1785–1866)
Rich and Poor

Sometimes the poor man did not even have the mixed blessing of the daylight.

Wednesday, 18 May, 1870

Went down to the Bath Flower Show in Sydney College Gardens. Found the first train going down was an Excursion train and took a ticket for it. The carriage was nearly full. In the Box tunnel, as there was no lamp, the people began to strike foul brimstone matches and hand them to each other all down the carriage. All the time we were in the tunnel these lighted matches

[20]

were travelling from hand to hand in the darkness. Each match lasted the length of the carriage and the red ember was thrown out of the opposite window, by which time another lighted match was seen travelling down the carriage. The carriage was chock full of brimstone fumes, the windows both nearly shut, and by the time we got out of the tunnel I was almost suffocated.

Revd. Francis Kilvert, *Diary*

Despite the attempt at separating passengers into classes, trains do throw together all manner of unlikely travelling companions. Whether in Britain or abroad, not everyone approves of the resulting chaos.

Trains sum up, to my mind, all the fogs and muddled misery of the nineteenth century. They constitute, in fact, so many slums on wheels.

Osbert Sitwell, *Penny Foolish, By Train*, 1935

'I say that there is not one rule of right living which these *te-rains* do not cause us to break. We sit, for example, side by side with all castes and peoples.'

Rudyard Kipling, *Kim*, 1901

What is Stephen Spender's poem about ? Schoolboys who complained that poetry was out of touch with reality, used to be offered 'The Express' as an example of the poetic treatment of an everyday subject. But a lot of ink has been spilled by those who, knowing Spender's left-wing politics in the Thirties and seizing on the word 'manifesto', have argued that the whole thing is a symbolic description of the progress of Communism. Whatever the underlying meaning of the poem, it has taken a hundred years for the train to sink so deeply into human consciousness that it can re-emerge transformed into a series of enigmatic metaphors.

THE EXPRESS

After the first powerful plain manifesto
The black statement of pistons, without more fuss
But gliding like a queen, she leaves the station.
Without bowing and with restrained unconcern
She passes the houses which humbly crowd outside,
The gasworks and at last the heavy page
Of death, printed by gravestones in the cemetery.
Beyond the town there lies the open country
Where, gathering speed, she acquires mystery,
The luminous self-possession of ships on ocean.
It is now she begins to sing – at first quite low
Then loud, and at last with a jazzy madness –
The song of her whistle screaming at curves,
Of deafening tunnels, brakes, innumerable bolts.
And always light, aerial, underneath
Goes the elate metre of her wheels.
Steaming through metal landscape on her lines
She plunges new eras of wild happiness
Where speed throws up strange shapes, broad curves
And parallels clean like the steel of guns.
At last, further than Edinburgh or Rome,
Beyond the crest of the world, she reaches night
Where only a low streamline brightness
Of phosphorus on the tossing hills is white.
Ah, like a comet through flames she moves entranced
Wrapt in her music no bird song, no, nor bough
Breaking with honey buds, shall ever equal.

Stephen Spender, 1934

From class and politics to . . . sex. But, surprisingly, sex does not so much raise its ugly head as timidly peep round the compartment door. The train is an obvious and potent sex-symbol, yet as such it has scarcely begun to be exploited. The next four pieces point the way.

At midday, Ernestine ... heard the faint, far-away *chuff-chuff* of the train from Italy. Trains were a novelty to Ernestine; they were fascinating, unknown, terrible. What were they like as they came tearing their way through the valley, plunging be.ween the mountains as if not even the mountains could stop them? When she saw the dark, flat breast of the engine, so bare, so powerful, hurled as it were towards her, she felt a weakness – she could have sunk to the earth. And yet she must look.

Katherine Mansfield, *Father and the Girls*, 1923

NIGHT EXPRESS

Night falls. The dark expresses
Roll back their iron scissors to commence
Precision of the wheels' elision
From whose dark serial jabber sparks
Swing swaying through the mournful capitals

And in these lighted cages sleep
With open eyes the passengers
Each committed to his private folly,
On hinges of wanhope the long
Sleeping shelves of men and women,
A library of maggots dreaming, rolls.

Some retiring to their sleeping past,
On clicking pillows feel the flickering peep
Of lighted memories, keys slipped in grooves
Parted like lips receiving or resisting kisses.
Pillars of smoke expend futurity.

This is how it is for me, for you
It must be different lying awake to hear
At a garden's end the terrible club-foot
Crashing among iron spars, the female shrieks,
Love-song of steel and the consenting night.

[23]

To feel the mocking janitor, sleep,
Shake now and wake to lean there
On a soft elbow seeing where we race
A whiplash curving outwards to the stars,
A glowing coal to light the lamps of space.

Lawrence Durrell

THE SHUNTERS

The colour of grief, and thoroughly tame,
the shunters slave on silver parallels.
Propitious their proletarian numbers.
Only posh expresses sport proper names.

In the tired afternoon drizzle, their smoke
fades into industrial England.
Governed by levers, hearing clanking chains,
how can a smudge of engines run amok ?

Rain drags darkness down where shunters work
the blank gloom below hoardings, dejected sheds,
below yellow squares in backs of tenements
whilst, resigned, charcoal trucks clash and jerk.

A prince is due. Like victims shunters wait
meekly – *The Red Dragon* ? *The Devon Belle* ?
A crash of lights. Four o'clock schoolboys gape
over the bridge, inarticulate.

Later, late, again, far their echoes rage;
hurt, plaintive wheels; hyphenated trucks;
sexual cries from funnels – all punctuate
the night, a despair beyond language.

Dannie Abse

The great trains are going out all over Europe, one by
one, but still, three times a week, the Orient Express
thunders superbly over the 1400 miles of glittering
steel between Istanbul and Paris.

Under the arc-lights, the long-chassied German
locomotive panted quietly with the laboured breath of

[24]

a dragon dying of asthma. Each heavy breath seemed certain to be the last. Then came another. Wisps of steam rose from the couplings between the carriages and died quickly in the warm August air. The Orient Express was the only live train in the ugly, cheaply architectured burrow that is Istanbul's main station. The trains on the other lines were engineless and unattended – waiting for tomorrow. Only track No. 3, and its platform, throbbed with the tragic poetry of departure.

The heavy bronze cipher on the side of the dark blue coach said, COMPAGNIE INTERNATIONALE DES WAGON-LITS ET DES GRANDS EXPRESS EUROPÉENS. Above the cipher, fitted into metal slots, was a flat iron sign that announced, in black capitals on white, ORIENT EXPRESS, and underneath, in three lines:

ISTANBUL   THESSALONIKI   BEOGRAD

VENEZIA   MILAN

LAUSANNE   PARIS

James Bond gazed vaguely at one of the most romantic signs in the world. For the tenth time he looked at his watch. 8.51. His eyes went back to the sign. All the towns were spelled in the language of the country except MILAN. Why not MILANO ? Bond took out his handkerchief and wiped his face. Where the hell was the girl ? Had she been caught ? Had she had second thoughts? Had he been too rough with her last night, or rather this morning, in the great bed ?

Ian Fleming, *From Russia With Love*, 1957

What goes on at the bottom of Robert Service's garden is a bit more straightforward than what happens at the bottom of Lawrence Durrell's. Ian Fleming regrets the decline of the great expresses. For Robert Service, writing a little earlier, the expresses are still going strong, but his James Bond days are over.

CONTINENTAL TRAINS

World-famous trains my garden pass
  A dozen times a day;
Long and luxurious of class,
  Mid palms they push their way;
And some are bound for Italy,
  While some are sped for Spain;
And some for Berlin on the Spree,
  Or Paris on the Seine.

And as I watch them puff and pull,
  My travel feet I feel;
They itch for Zurich and Stamboul,
  For Naples and Seville.
Sleek conjurers of bright desire,
  Of up-and-going pains,
Imagination fast to fire
  Are Continental trains.

The sleeping and the dining cars
  Superbly pass me by,
With richness that the pocket bars
  From scribblers such as I.
My garden where the roses foam
  With love I live amid,
But oh! I dream of golden Rome,
  And glamorous Madrid.

Yet with my blanket on my back
  In youth I beat my way
Along a lousy railway track
  From Maine to Monterey.
Alas! What sybarites are we,
  As life's soft twilight wanes,
Who seek the scented luxury
  Of Continental trains!

Robert Service

Stations

You cannot have railways without trains. You cannot have trains without stations. G. K. Chesterton, as we have already seen, found 'quietude and consolation' in stations, while Ruskin only wanted to escape as soon as possible. The Ruskin attitude seems to be the commoner. I suppose that stations give rise to melancholy and thoughts of suicide because, for those who have not got the fare or are restrained (or imagine themselves to be) by job, family, or other hostages to fortune, they represent unattainable adventure and escape.

Angoisse des gares (station anxiety) existed long before Cyril Connolly, using the pseudonym Palinurus, anatomized it so elegantly – though some of his alleged causes are questionable.

Angoisse des Gares: A particularly violent form of Angst. Bad when we meet someone at the station, much worse when we are seeing them off; not present when departing oneself, but unbearable when arriving in London, if only from a day in Brighton. Since all Angst is identical, we may learn something from these station-fears: Arrival-Angst is closely connected with guilt, with the dread of something terrible having happened during our absence. Death of parents. Entry of bailiffs. Flight of loved one. Sensations worse at arriving in the evening than the morning, and much worse at Victoria and Waterloo than at Paddington.

Partly this is due to my having gone abroad every vacation and, therefore, to returning to London with guilt-feelings about having spent all my money, or not written to parents, and to endless worry over work and debts. Going to London as a schoolboy was a jaunt, as an undergraduate an ordeal, a surrender to justice. Later the trips abroad lengthened, and returns were painful because of household worries replacing former debts, and through a particularly strong guilt-feeling about not being at work, or at having been out-distanced by successful stay-at-home friends.

But this is not all, for much of our anxiety is caused by the horror of London itself; of its hideous entrails as seen from the southern approaches, its high cost of living, its embodiment of ugly and unnatural urban existence. When living in France, I began to feel the same way about Paris, though it has none of the same associations. I deduce, therefore, that though it is wrong for us to live and work in great cities, it is also wrong to live away from them *without working*.

Angst begins at Reading (for Paddington), Brookwood, the London Necropolis (for Waterloo), the tunnels through the North Downs (for Victoria), or even in Paris, when we see the grisly English faces homeward bound at the Gare du Nord. First-class or third makes no difference. 'They' will get you, Palinurus, 'they' aren't taken in.

Palinurus, *The Unquiet Grave*, 1945

Anthony Trollope points to another cause of station anxiety – the apparent chaos and confusion prevailing at large junctions. The Victorians believed that 'a great genius of order' presided over more than mere railway stations. Today, alas, we have lost their confidence and certainty.

Not a minute passes without a train going here or there, some rushing by without noticing Tenway in the least, crashing through like flashes of substantial lightning, and others stopping, disgorging and taking up passengers by the hundreds. Men and women, – especially the men, for the women knowing their ignorance are generally willing to trust to the pundits of the place, – look doubtful, uneasy, and bewildered. But they all do get properly placed and unplaced, so that the spectator at last acknowledges that over all this apparent chaos there is presiding a great genius of order.

Anthony Trollope, *The Prime Minister*, 1876

John Davidson, Dylan Thomas, and Anthony Thwaite each write about those people who spend their time on stations, among travellers, ironically because they have nowhere to go.

> But orchards lit with golden lamps,
> Or purple moor, or nutbrown stream,
> Or mountains where the morn encamps
> Frequent no station-loafer's dream:
> A breed of folk forlorn that seem
> The heirs of disappointment, cast
> By fate to be the preacher's theme,
> To hunger daily and to fast,
> And sink to helpless indigence at last.

From early morn they hang about
The bookstall, the refreshment-room;
They pause and think, as if in doubt
Which train to go by; now assume
A jaunty air, and now in gloom
They take the platform for a stage
And pace it, meditating doom –
Their own, the world's; in baffled rage
Condemning still the imperceptive age.

John Davidson, *Railway Stations, 11 Liverpool Street Station*

There will be women, beckoning without moving, over their cold coffee; old, anonymous men with snuff on their cheeks, trembling over tea; quiet men expecting no one from the trains they wait for eagerly every hour; women who have come to run away, to take a train to St. Ives or Liverpool or anywhere, but who know they will never take any train and are drinking cups of tea and saying to themselves, 'I could be catching the twelve o'clock but I'll wait for the quarter past'; women from the country with dozens of children coming undone; shop girls, office girls, street girls, people who have nothing worse to do, all the unhappy, happy in chains, bewildered foreign men and women in the station buffet of the city I know from cover to cover.

Dylan Thomas, *Adventures in the Skin Trade*, 1955

SUNDAY AFTERNOONS

On Sunday afternoons
In winter, snow in the air,
People sit thick as birds
In the station buffet-bar.
They know one another.
Some exchange a few words
But mostly they sit and stare
At the urns and the rock buns.

Not many trains today.
Not many are waiting for trains
Or waiting for anything
Except for the time to pass.
The fug is thick on the glass
Beyond which, through honks and puffing,
An express shrugs and strains
To sidings not far away.

Here no one is saying goodbye:
Tears, promises to write,
Journeys, are not for them.
Here there are other things
To mull over, till the dark brings
Its usual burdensome
Thoughts of a place for the night,
A bit of warm and dry.

On Sunday afternoons
The loudspeaker has little to say
Of wherever the few trains go.
Not many are travellers.
But few are as still as these
Who sit here out of the snow,
Passing the time away
Till the night begins.

Anthony Thwaite, from *The Owl in the Tree*, 1963

§

John Wain's protagonist, Geary, in The Smaller Sky
*(1967), is no down-and-out or tramp; he is a respectable
boffin who has decided that Paddington Station contains
everything necessary for a civilized existence. Logically,
there seems to be no reason why his scheme should not work.
But . . .*

'Would you mind telling me,' Robinson went on
determinedly, 'how long you've been on this station?'

'Nine days,' said Geary. . . .

'Look, let me get this straight,' said Robinson. 'You spend your nights in the station hotel and your days walking about on the platforms?'

'Sometimes walking, sometimes just sitting. And I have my meals in the different refreshment rooms. I'm getting to be quite an authority on them. . . .'

'If every large railway station had a hundred people living on it permanently, and you'd always been used to the idea, it wouldn't seem irrational at all,' said Geary. 'You accept far more arbitrary things, every day of your life.'

John Wain's Paddington and W. H. Auden's Gare du Midi are related – large metropolitan termini where it is precisely what seems most ordinary that is the most menacing.

GARE DU MIDI

A nondescript express from the South,
Crowds round the ticket barrier, a face
To welcome which the mayor has not contrived
Bugles or braid: something about the mouth
Distracts the stray look with alarm and pity.
Snow is falling. Clutching a little case,
He walks out briskly to infect a city
Whose terrible future may just have arrived.

W. H. Auden, 1938

Stations are not only places where we arrive or even, paradoxically, spend our days in immobility; they are also starting-points for all manner of journeys, humdrum and exotic. In this piece by E. M. Forster, 'the pylons of Euston' means the noble, pedimented archways, since demolished. Even today, some seventy years after this was written, there still exist guards who might, if they came across her, place Mrs Munt in a first-class carriage.

Like many others who have lived long in a great capital, she had strong feelings about the various railway termini. They are our gates to the glorious and the unknown. Through them we pass out into adventure and sunshine, to them, alas! we return. In Paddington all Cornwall is latent and the remoter west; down the inclines of Liverpool Street lie fenlands and the illimitable Broads; Scotland is through the pylons of Euston; Wessex behind the poised chaos of Waterloo. Italians realize this, as is natural; those of them who are so unfortunate as to serve as waiters in Berlin call the Anhalt Bahnhof the Stazione d'Italia, because by it they must return to their homes. And he is a chilly Londoner who does not endow his stations with some personality, and extend to them, however shyly, the emotions of fear and love.

To Margaret – I hope that it will not set the reader against her – the station of King's Cross had always suggested Infinity. Its very situation – withdrawn a little behind the facile splendours of St. Pancras – implied a comment on the materialism of life. Those two great arches, colourless, indifferent, shouldering between them an unlovely clock, were fit portals for some eternal adventure, whose issue might be prosperous, but would certainly not be expressed in the ordinary language of prosperity. If you think this ridiculous, remember that it is not Margaret who is telling you about it; and let me hasten to add that they were in plenty of time for the train; and that Mrs Munt, though she took a second-class ticket, was put by the guard into a first (only two seconds on the train, one smoking and the other babies – one cannot be expected to travel with babies) . . .

E. M. Forster, *Howards End*, 1910

P. G. Wodehouse is making the same point as E. M. Forster, with a rather lighter touch.

'To one like myself', said Lord Ickenham, 'who living in Hampshire, gets out of the metropolis, when he is fortunate enough to get into it, *via* Waterloo, there is something very soothing in the note of refined calm which Paddington strikes. At Waterloo, all is hustle and bustle, and the society tends to be mixed. Here a leisured peace prevails, and you get only the best people – cultured men accustomed to mingling with basset hounds and women in tailored suits who look like horses.'

P. G. Wodehouse, *Uncle Fred in the Springtime*, 1939

Approached in the right spirit, big stations can yield all manner of pleasant experiences. That unattended bag need not contain the wherewithal to 'infect a city'; it may reveal a healthy baby of impeccable pedigree.

JACK. The late Mr Thomas Cardew, an old gentleman of a very charitable and kindly disposition, found me, and gave me the name of Worthing, because he happened to have a first-class ticket for Worthing in his pocket at the time. Worthing is a place in Sussex. It is a seaside resort.

LADY BRACKNELL. Where did the charitable gentleman who had a first-class ticket for this seaside resort find you?

JACK [*gravely*]. In a hand-bag.

LADY BRACKNELL. A hand-bag?

JACK [*very seriously*]. Yes, Lady Bracknell. I was in a hand-bag – a somewhat large, black leather hand-bag, with handles to it – an ordinary hand-bag in fact.

LADY BRACKNELL. In what locality did this Mr James, or Thomas, Cardew come across this ordinary hand-bag?

JACK. In the cloak-room at Victoria Station. It was given to him in mistake for his own.

LADY BRACKNELL. The cloak-room at Victoria Station ?

JACK. Yes. The Brighton line.

LADY BRACKNELL. The line is immaterial. Mr Worthing, I confess I feel somewhat bewildered by what you have just told me. To be born, or at any rate bred, in a hand-bag, whether it had handles or not, seems to me to display a contempt for the ordinary decencies of family life that reminds one of the worst excesses of the French Revolution. And I presume you know what that unfortunate movement led to ? As for the particular locality in which the hand-bag was found, a cloak-room at a railway station might serve to conceal a social indiscretion – has probably, indeed, been used for that purpose before now – but it could hardly be regarded as an assured basis for a recognized position in good society.

Oscar Wilde, *The Importance of Being Earnest*, 1895

Your fellow-travellers need not always be secret agents or screaming babies.

> There is one memory God can never break,
> There is one splendour more than all the pain,
> There is one secret that shall never die,
> Star-crowned I stand and sing, for that hour's sake.
> In Freiburg station, waiting for a train,
> I saw a bishop with puce gloves go by.
>
> Rupert Brooke, *In Freiburg Station*, 1912

That soldier need not be an enemy, but a human being with a liking for flowers and romance.

Alexandria Main Station: midnight. A deathly heavy dew. The noise of wheels cracking the slime-slithering pavements. Yellow pools of phosphorous light, and corridors of darkness like tears in the dull brick façade of a stage set. Policemen in the shadows. Standing against an insanitary brick wall to kiss her goodbye. She is going for a week, but in the panic, half-asleep I can see that she may never come back. The soft resolute kiss and the bright eyes fill me with emptiness. From the dark platform comes the crunch of rifle-butts and the clicking of Bengali. A detail of Indian troops on some routine transfer to Cairo. It is only as the train begins to move, and as the figure at the window, dark against the darkness, lets go of my hand, that I feel Melissa is really leaving; feel everything that is inexorably denied – the long pull of the train into the silver light reminds me of the sudden long pull of the vertebrae of her white back turning in bed. 'Melissa', I call out but the giant sniffing of the engine blots out all sound. She begins to tilt, to curve and slide; and quick as a scene-shifter the station packs away advertisement after advertisement, stacking them in the darkness. I stand as if marooned on an iceberg. Beside me a tall Sikh shoulders the rifle he has stopped with a rose. The shadowy figure is sliding away down the steel rails into the darkness; a final lurch and the train pours away down a tunnel, as if turned to liquid.

Lawrence Durrell, Justine, 1966

If you have never travelled by train before, you are unlikely to notice details like gloves and roses. Even some people who have made thousands of journeys still think of trains as 'the work of devils'. Just as Dickens makes the railway a minor but persistent thread throughout Dombey and Son, *so Kipling uses it for one of his leitmotivs in* Kim.

They entered the fort-like railway station, black in the end of the night; the electrics sizzling over the goods yard where they handle the heavy Northern grain-traffic.

'This is the work of devils!' said the lama, recoiling from the hollow echoing darkness, the glimmer of rails between the masonry platforms, and the maze of girders above. He stood in a gigantic stone hall paved, it seemed, with the sheeted dead – third-class passengers who had taken their tickets overnight and were sleeping in the waiting-rooms. All hours of the twenty-four are alike to Orientals, and their passenger traffic is regulated accordingly.

'This is where the fire-carriages come. One stands behind that hole' – Kim pointed to the ticket-office – 'who will give thee a paper to take thee to Umballa.'

Rudyard Kipling, Kim, 1901

For children stations are sheer paradise.

Never before had any one of them been at a station, except for the purpose of catching trains – or perhaps waiting for them – and always with grown-ups in attendance, grown-ups who were not themselves interested in stations, except as places from which they wished to get away.

Never before had they passed close enough to a signal-box to be able to notice the wires, and to hear the mysterious 'ping, ping', followed by the strong, firm clicking of machinery.

The very sleepers on which the rails lay were a delightful path to travel by – just far enough apart to serve as the stepping-stones in a game of foaming torrents hastily organized by Bobbie.

Then to arrive at the station, not through the booking office, but in a freebooting sort of way by the sloping end of the platform. This in itself was joy.

Joy, too, it was to peep into the porters' room, where the lamps are, and the Railway almanac on the wall, and one porter half asleep behind a paper.

There were a great many crossing lines at the station; some of them just ran into a yard and stopped short, as though they were tired of business and meant to retire for good. Trucks stood on the rails here, and on one side was a great heap of coal.

E. Nesbit, *The Railway Children*, 1906

Stations can be in London or abroad; familiar or strange; friendly or hostile; Alexandria or . . . Adlestrop.

What is it about 'Adlestrop'? Edward Thomas wrote better poems. 'Adlestrop' is, in itself, no more than a pleasant Georgian vignette. It moves us today because it is totally of the past. What was a simple moment of happiness for Thomas is, for us, utterly unattainable. Thomas was killed in Flanders; steam engines have ceased to run; Adlestrop Station has been closed; farmers no longer build haycocks; passengers in their insulated coaches can no longer hear birdsong. Schoolchildren, struggling with the poem for O-levels, are directed to a pseudo-rustic bus-shelter in the middle of Adlestrop village where, surrounded by obscene graffiti, the poem is inscribed on a small plaque.

ADLESTROP

Yes, I remember Adlestrop –
The name, because one afternoon
Of heat the express-train drew up there
Unwontedly. It was late June.

The steam hissed. Someone cleared his throat.
No one left and no one came
On the bare platform. What I saw
Was Adlestrop – only the name

And willows, willow-herb, and grass,
And meadowsweet, and haycocks dry,
No whit less still and lonely fair
Than the high cloudlets in the sky.

And for that minute a blackbird sang
Close by, and round him, mistier,
Farther and farther, all the birds
Of Oxfordshire and Gloucestershire.

Edward Thomas, 1915

NOT ADLESTROP

Not Adlestrop, no – besides, the name
hardly matters. Nor did I languish in June heat.
Simply, I stood, too early, on the empty platform,
and the wrong train came in slowly, surprised, stopped.
Directly facing me, from a window,
a very, *very* pretty girl leaned out.

When I, all instinct,
stared at her, she, all instinct, inclined her head away
as if she'd divined the much married life in me,
or as if she might spot, up platform,
some unlikely familiar.

THE TRAIN

For my part, under the clock, I continued
my scrutiny with unmitigated pleasure.
And she knew it, she certainly knew it, and would not
glance at me in the silence of not Adlestrop.

Only when the train heaved noisily, only
when it jolted, when it slid away, only *then*,
daring and secure, she smiled back at my smile,
and I, daring and secure, waved back at her waving.
And so it was, all the way down the hurrying platform
as the train gathered atrocious speed
towards Oxfordshire or Gloucestershire.

Dannie Abse, 1970

*The connection between Dannie Abse's poem and Edward
Thomas's is that they are both about irretrievable moments. Robert Graves rounds off the Adlestrop theme and
indicates another ingredient in the appeal of Edward
Thomas's poem – the sense of an opportunity offered, and
not taken, to change the whole course of our lives.*

THE NEXT TIME

And that inevitable accident
  On the familiar journey – roughly reckoned
By miles and shillings – in a cramped compartment
  Between a first hereafter and a second ?

And when we passengers are given two hours,
  The wheels failing once more at Somewhere-
    Nowhere,
To climb out, stretch our legs and pick wild flowers –
  Suppose that this time I elect to stay there ?

Robert Graves

*No Oxford Book on railway travel would be complete
without a couple of references to Oxford's own station.
Here are two almost seventy years apart. I have a hunch
that, while Max Beerbohm would have felt quite at home
with the cosmopolitan* tohu-bohu *or* hotch-potch *to be
met on Oxford Station today, Professor Rowse might be
happier in the world of Zuleika Dobson.*

That old bell, presage of a train, had just sounded
through Oxford station; and the undergraduates who
were waiting there, gay figures in tweed or flannel,
moved to the margin of the platform and gazed idly
up the line. Young and careless, in the glow of the
afternoon sunshine, they struck a sharp note of incongruity with the worn boards they stood on, with the
fading signals and grey eternal walls of that antique
station, which, familiar to them and insignificant, does
yet whisper to the tourist the last enchantments of the
Middle Age.

Max Beerbohm, Zuleika Dobson, 1911

OXFORD STATION

    See that man standing on the platform
    Hat in hand, west wind in his hair,
    Back to the passengers waiting for the train,
    A look of some disdain for the nondescripts,
    Ruffling squalid newspapers, chewing,
    Chattering and shacking up with each other,
    Acne'd girls and pimpled, graceless youths:

All the *tohu-bohu* of Eastern Europe,
And odds and ends from Asia, Africa.
Impatiently he awaits the signal
When a cat cautiously crosses the track:
He is alarmed for an animal
Self-contained and lithe, beautiful and free.
An engine approaches, across the breast-plate
OMOO – he recognises the signal
From a fellow-spirit, Melville,
Restless and ranging, like himself
Unrecognised by the herd, solitary
And free.

A. L. Rowse, from *The Road to Oxford*, 1978

A. L. Rowse's mention of Melville (Omoo was an early novel of his) provides a splendid excuse for introducing – from Moby Dick *of all places – the ultimate railway metaphor.*

Come, Ahab's compliments to ye; come and see if you can swerve me. Swerve me ? ye cannot swerve me, else swerve yourselves ! man has ye there. Swerve me ? The path to my fixed purpose is laid with iron rails, whereon my soul is grooved to run. Over unsounded gorges, through the rifled hearts of mountains, under torrents' beds, unerringly I rush ! Naught's an obstacle, naught's an angle to the iron way !

Herman Melville, *Moby Dick*, 1851

Railway Staff

Trains and stations do not run themselves – yet. They need man, the ghost in the machine, to operate them. One of the first of these, in fiction at any rate, was Mr Toodle, the engine-driver, from . . .Dombey and Son. With what casual brilliance Dickens tosses in what is probably the first use of the expression 'train of ideas' since the advent of the railways gave it new resonance.

'You see, my boys and gals,' said Mr Toodle, looking round upon his family, 'wotever you're up to in a honest way, it's my opinion as you can't do better than be open. If you find yourselves in cuttings or in tunnels, don't you play no secret games. Keep your whistles going, and let's know where you are.'

The rising Toodles set up a shrill murmur, expressive of their resolution to profit by the paternal advice.

'But what makes you say this along of Rob, father ?' asked his wife, anxiously.

'Polly, old 'ooman,' said Mr Toodle, 'I don't know as I said it partickler along o' Rob, I'm sure. I starts light with Rob only; I comes to a branch; I takes on what I finds there; and a whole train of ideas gets coupled on to him, afore I knows where I am, or where they comes from. What a Junction a man's thoughts is,' said Mr Toodle, 'to-be-sure !'

Charles Dickens, Dombey and Son, 1846–8

As we have already seen, Thoreau had his doubts about the usefulness of railways. But he was second to none in his admiration of men like the snow-plough crew. Not so long ago in Britain platelayers did twelve-hour stints standing beside the tracks in fog, placing and removing detonators. Even today passengers may glimpse, exposed to all weathers, shunters with their poles, or men raking ballast, or others with spiked sticks putting litter into wicker baskets. Such figures still seem, in that Wordsworthian phrase, to 'occupy an outside place in the universe'.

I am less affected by their heroism who stood up for half-an-hour in the front line at Buena Vista, than by the steady and cheerful valour of the men who inhabit the snow-plough for their winter quarters; who have not merely the three o'clock in the morning courage which Bonaparte thought was the rarest, but whose courage does not go to rest so early, who go to sleep only when the storm sleeps or the sinews of their iron steed are frozen.

On this morning of the Great Snow, perchance, which is still raging and chilling men's blood, I hear the muffled tone of their engine bell from out of the fog-bank of their chilled breath, which announces that the cars *are coming*, without long delay, notwithstanding the veto of a New England north-east snow-storm, and I behold the ploughmen covered with snow and rime, their heads peering above the mould-board which is turning down other than daisies and the nests of field-mice, like boulders of the Sierra Nevada, that occupy an outside place in the universe.

Henry David Thoreau, *Walden, or Life in the Woods,* 1854

While on the subject of heroism, we must have one representative of the Casey Jones type; and who better than Conductor Bradley, whose deed was doubtless as noble as Whittier's verses about it are splendidly awful?

CONDUCTOR BRADLEY

A railway conductor who lost his life in an accident on
a Connecticut railway, 9 May 1873.

Conductor Bradley, (always may his name
Be said with reverence!) as the swift doom came,
Smitten to death, a crushed and mangled frame,

Sank, with the brake he grasped just where he stood
To do the utmost that a brave man could,
And die, if needful, as a true man should.

Men stooped above him; women dropped their tears
On that poor wreck beyond all hopes and fears,
Lost in the strength and glory of his years.

What heard they? Lo! the ghastly lips of pain,
Dead to all thought save duty's, moved again:
'Put out the signals for the other train!'

No nobler utterance since the world began
From lips of saint or martyr ever ran,
Electric, through the sympathies of man.

Ah me! how poor and noteless seem to this
The sick-bed dramas of self-consciousness,
Our sensual fears of pain and hopes of bliss!

Oh, grand, supreme endeavour! Not in vain
That last brave act of failing tongue and brain!
Freighted with life the downward rushing train,

Following the wrecked one, as wave follows wave,
Obeyed the warning which the dead lips gave.
Others he saved, himself he could not save.

Nay, the lost life *was* saved. He is not dead
Who in his record still the earth shall tread
With God's clear aureole shining round his head.

We bow as in the dust, with all our pride
Of virtue dwarfed the noble deed beside.
God give us grace to live as Bradley died!

John Greenleaf Whittier

*At first sight Finnigin may not appear to be a hero in the
Conductor Bradley mould. But I am not so sure. Was it
not heroic for a half-educated man to sit up all night
learning the virtues of précis the hard way? And at the
end of it did he not produce one of the noblest utterances
since the world began? God give us grace to write as
Finnigin did!*

FINNIGIN TO FLANNIGAN

Superintendent was Flannigan;
Boss av the siction wuz Finnigin;
Whiniver the kyars got offen the thrack,
An' muddled up things t' th' divil an' back,
Finnigin writ it to Flannagan,
After the wrick wuz all on ag'in;
   That is, this Finnigin
   Reported to Flannigan.

Whin Finnigin furst writ to Flannigan,
He writed tin pages – did Finnigin,
An' he tould jist how the smash occurred;
Full many a tajus blunderin' wurrd
Did Finnigin write to Flannigan
After the cars had gone on ag'in.
   That was how Finnigin
   Reported to Flannigan.

Now Flannigan knowed more than Finnigin –
He'd more idjucation, had Flannigan;
An' it wore 'm clane an' complately out
To tell what Finnigin writ about
In his writin' to Muster Flannigan.
So he writed back to Finnigin:
   'Don't do sich a sin ag'in;
   Make 'em brief, Finnigin !'

When Finnigin got this from Flannigan,
He blushed rosy rid, did Finnigin;
An' he said: 'I'll gamble a whole month's pa-ay
That it will be minny and minny a da-ay
Befoore Sup'rintindint – that's Flannigan –
Gets a whack at this very same sin ag'in.
   From Finnigin to Flannigan
   Repoorts won't be long ag'in.'

*

Wan da-ay, on the siction av Finnigin,
On the road sup'rintinded by Flannigan,
A rail giv way on a bit av a curve,
An' some kyars went off as they made the swerve.
'There's nobody hurted', sez Finnigin,
'But repoorts must be made to Flannigan.'
    An' he winked at McGorrigan,
    As married a Finnigin.

He wuz shantyin' thin, wuz Finnigin,
As minny a railroader's been ag'in,
An' the shmoky ol' lamp wuz burnin' bright
In Finnigin's shanty all that night –
Bilin' down his repoort was Finnigin!
An' he writed this here: 'Muster Flannigan:
    Off ag'in, on ag'in,
    Gone ag'in – Finnigin.'

S. W. Gillinan

§

From the heroic to the mundane. There follow four arrivals at sleepy rural stations. Is there a hint of irony in the Arnold Bennett? I do not think so. More than half a century ago such class distinctions really were as clear cut and taken for granted.

As soon as the doors had banged in a fusillade and the engine whistled, a young porter came and, having exchanged civilities with Harry, picked up Edwin's bag. This porter's face and demeanour showed perfect content. His slight yet eager smile and his quick movements seemed to be saying: 'It is natural and proper that I should salute you and carry your bag while you walk free. You are gentlemen by divine right, and by the same right I am a railway porter and happy.' To watch the man at his job gave positive pleasure, and it was extraordinarily reassuring – reassuring about everything.

Arnold Bennett, *These Twain*, 1916

Sometimes the staff of the local station were seen as little more than additional domestic servants.

Ten minutes late, in the hot evening sunshine, my train bustled contentedly along between orchards and hop gardens, jolted past the signal-box, puffed importantly under the bridge, and slowed up at Baldock Wood. The station was exactly the same as usual and I was very pleased to see it again. I was back from Ballboro' for the summer holidays. As I was going forward to the guard's van to identify my trunk and my wooden play-box, the station-master (who, in those days, wore a top-hat and a baggy black frock-coat) saluted me respectfully. Aunt Evelyn always sent him a turkey at Christmas.

Siegfried Sassoon, *Memoirs of a Fox-Hunting Man*, 1928

Even sixty years ago not all railwaymen kotowed to the gentry. Aldous Huxley's guard is alive and well and working many trains up and down the country.

The train came bumpingly to a halt. Here was Camlet at last. Denis jumped up, crammed his hat over his eyes, deranged his pile of baggage, leaned out of the window and shouted for a porter, seized a bag in either hand, and had to put them down again in order to open the door. When at last he had safely bundled himself and his baggage on to the platform, he ran up the train towards the van.

'A bicycle, a bicycle!' he said breathlessly to the guard. He felt himself a man of action. The guard paid no attention, but continued methodically to hand out, one by one, the packages labelled to Camlet. 'A bicycle!'

Denis repeated. 'A green machine, cross-framed, name of Stone. S-T-O-N-E.'

'All in good time, sir,' said the guard soothingly. He was a large, stately man with a naval beard. One pictured him at home, drinking tea, surrounded by a numerous family. It was in that tone that he must have spoken to his children when they were tiresome. 'All in good time, sir.' Denis's man of action collapsed, punctured.

Aldous Huxley, *Crome Yellow*, 1921

Just another arrival? Is it only because we know the story that the whole peaceful scene seems loaded with menace?

About five o'clock the carriage emptied, and I was left alone as I had hoped. I got out at the next station, a little place whose name I scarcely noted, set right in the heart of a bog. It reminded me of one of those forgotten little stations in the Karroo. An old station-master was digging in his garden, and with his spade over his shoulder sauntered to the train, took charge of a parcel, and went back to his potatoes. A child of ten received my ticket, and I emerged on a white road that straggled over the brown moor.

John Buchan, *The Thirty-Nine Steps*, 1915

And here is one more piece from the irresistible Railway Children. *Although her canvas is smaller, E. Nesbit has this much in common with Dickens and Kipling, that she perceives the value of the train as a theme and a symbol. It brings and it takes away. It is the machine that bears the god. It can be equally and impartially a source of sorrow or of happiness.*

The Porter told them many things that they had not known before – as, for instance, that the things that hook carriages together are called couplings, and that

the pipes like great serpents that hang over the couplings are meant to stop the train with.

'If you could get a holt of one o' them when the
train is going and pull 'em apart', said he, 'she'd stop
dead off with a jerk.'

'Who's she?' said Phyllis.

'The train, of course,' said the Porter. After that the
train was never again 'It' to the children.

'And you know the thing in the carriages where it
says on it, "Five pounds' fine for improper use". If you
was to improperly use that, the train 'ud stop.'

'And if you used it properly?' said Roberta.

'It 'ud stop just the same, I suppose', said he, 'but it
isn't proper use unless you're being murdered. There
was an old lady once – someone kidded her on it was a
refreshment-room bell, and she used it improper, not
being in danger of her life, though hungry, and when
the train stopped and the guard came along expecting
to find someone weltering in their last moments, she
says, "Oh, please, Mister, I'll take a glass of stout and
a bath bun", she says. And the train was seven minutes
behind her time as it was.'

§

*This is the inimitable Brian O'Nolan alias Myles na
Gopaleen alias Flann O'Brien. Apart from producing
astonishing novels, he ran a column in the* Irish Times *in
which he dealt with anything and everything, including
railways. Here he has his tongue firmly in his cheek.*

FOOTPLATE TOPICS

Coming back to the cognate subject of railway working,
I should not like it to be taken from my remarks a few
weeks ago that I would like to go down in railway
history as a 'full regulator man'. In my railway days
you would not always find me with the lever pulled

right up; still more rarely would you find me yielding to the temptation to work on the 'first port' and cut off late. Sometimes, when conditions suited, you would find me blowing down to reduce priming, but never when the design left me open to the danger of having my valve jammed open. And none knew better than I when to shut off my cylinder oil feed when drifting. I could write a book on how to economise on locomotive working in the present difficult times, but our self-opinionated and pig-headed railway bosses would probably ignore it.

Flann O'Brien, from *The Best of Myles*, 1968

Stockton & Darlington
Railway.
The Company's
COACH

CALLED THE

EXPERIMENT,

Which commenced Travelling on MONDAY, the 10th of OCTOBER, 1825, will continue to run from *Darlington* to *Stockton*, and from *Stockton* to *Darlington* every Day. [Sunday's excepted] setting off from the DEPOT at each place, at the times specified as under. (*&c.*)!——

ON MONDAY,

From Stockton at half-past 7 in the Morning, and will reach Darlington about half-past 9; the Coach will set off from the latter place on its return at 3 in the Afternoon, and reach Stockton about 5.

TUESDAY,

From Stockton at 3 in the Afternoon, and will reach Darlington about 5.

On the following Days, viz.——

WEDNESDAY, THURSDAY & FRIDAY,

From Darlington at half-past 7 in the Morning, and will reach Stockton about half-past 9; the Coach will set off from the latter place on its return at 3 in the Afternoon, and reach Darlington about 5.

SATURDAY,

From Darlington at 1 in the Afternoon, and will reach Stockton about 3.

Passengers to pay 1s. each, and will be allowed a Package of not exceeding 14lb. all above that weight to pay at the rate of 2d. per Stone extra. Carriage of small Parcels 3d. each. The Company will not be accountable for Parcels of above £5. Value, unless paid for as such.

Mr RICHARD PICKERSGILL at his Office in Commercial Street, Darlington; and Mr TULLY at Stockton, will for the present receive any Parcels and Book Passengers

The Journey

We have railways, trains, stations, and staff. Now we, the passengers, can fare forward. Almost infinite are the possible ways of spending the journey, the possible purposes of the journey, the possible outcomes. We can go far in the flesh; in the mind we can travel farther still.

Life is a railway journey.

John Davidson, from *The Testament of Sir Simon Simplex Concerning Automobilism*

Scott Fitzgerald here is saying in prose what John Davidson so succinctly states in verse.

A ride in a train can be a terrible, heavy-hearted, or comic thing; it can be a trial flight; it can be a prefiguration of another journey, just as a given day with a friend can be long, from the taste of hurry in the morning up to the realization of both being hungry and taking food together. Then comes the afternoon with the journey fading and dying, but quickening again at the end.

F. Scott Fitzgerald, *Tender is the Night*, 1939

But while life is a railway journey, Dickens, through Mr Dombey embittered by the premature loss of his son, reaches the inevitable conclusion that the train represents Death.

He [Mr Dombey] found no pleasure or relief in the journey. Tortured by these thoughts he carried monotony with him, through the rushing landscape, and hurried headlong, not through a rich and varied country, but a wilderness of blighted plans and

gnawing jealousies. The very speed at which the train
was whirled along mocked the swift course of the
young life that had been borne away so steadily and so
inexorably to its foredoomed end. The power that
forced itself upon its iron way – its own – defiant of all
paths and roads, piercing through the heart of every
obstacle, and dragging living creatures of all classes,
ages, and degrees behind it, was a type of the trium-
phant monster, Death.

Charles Dickens, *Dombey and Son*, 1846–8

*Stevenson's ride across America takes us away from
solemn thoughts of life and death, and raises the issue of
perspective. Especially journeying through a vast landscape, the traveller begins to have delusions of grandeur.
He sees the train and himself aboard it as important, and
everything else as trivial and insignificant.*

We were at sea – there is no other adequate expression –
on the plains of Nebraska. I made my observatory on
the top of a fruit-waggon, and sat by the hour upon
that perch to spy about me, and to spy in vain for
something new. It was a world almost without a feature;
an empty sky, an empty earth; front and back, the line
of railway stretched from horizon to horizon, like a
cue across a billiard-board; on either hand, the green
plain ran till it touched the skirts of heaven. Along the
track innumerable wild sunflowers, no bigger than a
crown-piece, bloomed in a continuous flower-bed;
grazing beasts were seen upon the prairie at all degrees
of distance and diminution; and now and again we
might perceive a few dots beside the railroad which
grew more and more distinct as we drew nearer till
they turned into wooden cabins, and then dwindled and
dwindled in our wake until they melted into their
surroundings, and we were once more alone upon the
billiard-board. The train toiled over this infinity like a

snail; and being the one thing moving, it was wonderful what huge proportions it began to assume in our regard. It seemed miles in length, and either end of it within but a step of the horizon.

Robert Louis Stevenson, *Across the Plains*, 1892

But the passenger should beware of getting ideas above his station. Within those little wooden dots live human beings who cultivate the sunflowers, tend the animals, and see the passing trains as minor diversions. Robert Frost gives the other side of the picture.

THE FIGURE IN THE DOORWAY or
On Being Looked At in a Train

The grade surmounted, we were riding high
Through level mountains nothing to the eye
But scrub oak, scrub oak and the lack of earth
That kept the oaks from getting any girth.
But as through the monotony we ran,
We came to where there was a living man.
His great gaunt figure filled his cabin door,
And had he fallen inward on the floor,
He must have measured to the further wall.
But we who passed were not to see him fall.
The miles and miles he lived from anywhere
Were evidently something he could bear.
He stood unshaken, and if grim and gaunt,
It was not necessarily from want.
He had the oaks for heating and for light.
He had a hen, he had a pig in sight.
He had a well, he had the rain to catch.
He had a ten-by-twenty garden patch.
Nor did he lack for common entertainment.
That I assume was what our passing train meant.
He could look at us in our diner eating,
And if so moved uncurl a hand in greeting.

Robert Frost

*It is all a question of one's point of view. Many people
know Frances Cornford's 'fat white woman'. Chesterton's
witty reply deserves to be better known.*

TO A FAT LADY SEEN FROM THE TRAIN

O why do you walk through the fields in gloves,
    Missing so much and so much ?
O fat white woman whom nobody loves,
Why do you walk through the fields in gloves,
When the grass is soft as the breast of doves
    And shivering-sweet to the touch ?
O why do you walk through the fields in gloves,
    Missing so much and so much ?

Frances Cornford

THE FAT WHITE WOMAN SPEAKS

Why do you rush through the fields in trains,
Guessing so much and so much ?
Why do you flash through the flowery meads,
Fat-headed poet that nobody reads;
And why do you know such a frightful lot
About people in gloves as such ?

And how the devil can you be sure,
Guessing so much and so much,
How do you know but what someone who loves
Always to see me in nice white gloves
At the end of the field you are rushing by,
Is waiting for his Old Dutch ?

G. K. Chesterton, from *New Poems*, 1932

§

*Looking out of the train window is rather like watching
live television. We are powerless to intervene in what we
see. In Agatha Christie's 4.50 from Paddington, Mrs
McGillicuddy witnesses a murder being committed on
board a train overtaking hers. Most of us do not see
murders, thank goodness; but whatever we see – a*

cricket-match, a couple making love, a family sharing a
meal – we feel it does not concern us. Similarly, the
players, the lovers, the diners ignore our train. It does not
occur to them that we exist. Yet no man is an island...

> ... one looks from the train
> And there is something, the same thing
> Behind everything: all these little villages,
> A passing woman, a field of grain,
> The man who says good-bye to his wife –
> A path through a wood full of lives, and the train
> Passing, after all unchangeable
> And not now ever to stop, like a heart.

Randall Jarrell, The Orient Express

The long train moves: we move in it along.
Like an old ballad, or an endless song,
It drones and wimbles its unwearied croon –
Croons, drones, and mumbles all the afternoon.

Towns with their fifty chimneys close and high,
Wreathed in great smoke between the earth and sky,
It hurtles through them, and you think it must
Halt – but it shrieks and sputters them with dust,
Cracks like a bullet through their big affairs,
Rushes the station-bridge, and disappears
Out to the suburb, laying bare
Each garden trimmed with pitiful care;
Children are caught at idle play,
Held a moment, and thrown away.
Nearly everyone looks round.
Some dignified inhabitant is found
Right in the middle of the commonplace –
Buttoning his trousers...

Harold Monro, from Journey

There was a drama outside Nis. At a road near the
track a crowd of people fought to look at a horse, still

in its traces and hitched to an overloaded wagon, lying dead on its side in a mud puddle in which the wagon was obviously stuck. I imagined its heart had burst when it tried to free the wagon. And it had just happened: children were calling to their friends, a man was dropping his bike and running back for a look, and farther along a man pissing against a fence was straining to see the horse. The scene was composed like a Flemish painting in which the pissing man was a vivid detail. The train, the window frame holding the scene for moments, made it a picture. The man at the fence flicks the last droplets from his penis and, tucking it in his baggy pants, begins to sprint; the picture is complete.

Paul Theroux, *The Great Railway Bazaar*, 1975

W. R. Rodgers regrets that his own younger self no longer responds to his greeting.

THE TRAIN

There with a screech stuck in her hair like a feather
She strikes through signals, sequels, stares, and
    significations
With equal squeal; scattering the stuck tons of
    thunder
In tunnels like tins staccato; alliterating
The laddering lights and escalatoring clatter till
At last she assonants free. The elbowing air
Ushers her on, cushions and repercussions her
In its indulgent hush. And always her weeping past
Wallabies wildly away in smokes and hang-
Overs of gloom across the long-ago fields that once
    were mine.
Long ago ? No. The cataract still hangs
In tatters as it did. On the same thong of air
The hawk impends. Still leans the lonely tree
Above the only lake, its ageing shade

Unwrinkled in the shaking glass. And still
The fountain eyelashes a stony stare.
All's as I left it, place and pose and weather
That once was willed for ever. Once again
I look out from the train,
I see the solemn child, and wave to it in vain.

W. R. Rodgers

When Scott Fitzgerald thinks of his youth, it is the trains that he remembers, because he was so happy in them.

One of my most vivid memories is of coming back West from prep school and later from college at Christmas time. Those who went farther than Chicago would gather in the old dim Union Station at six o'clock of a December evening, with a few Chicago friends, already caught up into their own holiday gaieties, to bid them a hasty good-bye. I remember . . . the long green tickets clasped tight in our gloved hands. And last the murky yellow cars of the Chicago, Milwaukee and St Paul railroad looking cheerful as Christmas itself on the tracks beside the gate.

When we pulled out into the winter night and the real snow, our snow, began to stretch out beside us and twinkle against the windows, and the dim lights of small Wisconsin stations moved by, a sharp wild brace came suddenly into the air. We drew in deep breaths of it as we walked back from dinner through the cold vestibules, unutterably aware of our identity with this country for one strange hour, before we melted indistinguishably into it again.

That's my Middle West – not the wheat or the prairies or the lost Swede towns, but the thrilling returning trains of my youth. . .

F. Scott Fitzgerald, *The Great Gatsby*, 1926

*Lawrence Durrell has twinkling snow, too, as he offers a
fascinating glimpse of the poet at work. The prose extract
is, well, prosaic. In the poem the same episode is transformed with 'the little train' perfectly embedded in its
centre.*

How eerie her arrival was; a light and wholly irrational
snowstorm of light flakes had started. The snow
melted as it touched the ground. You could hear the
train far away in the darkness somewhere, the mesh of
wheels and its little apologetic foghorn. An answering
bell somewhere in the station started to echo, started to
throb. Then in the further darkness of the hinterland,
upon the velvety screen of night, as if in response I
saw a sudden line of yellow lights moving slowly across
the skyline, softly tinkling as the whole chaplet came
slowly and sinuously down to the level of the plain.
The little station bell went mad now. It throbbed as
if it had a high temperature. I waited on the dark
platform with this very light snow – a mere swish-like
spray – caressing my neck. The train arrived with a
clamour and a final sprint, a rush. It came to rest in the
station; it was apparently empty. There was not even
a guard aboard. In my disappointment I was about to
turn away and set off back to Orta when at the very
end a carriage door opened, a bar of light fell on the
snowy platform, and Vega stepped out.

Lawrence Durrell, *A Smile in the Mind's Eye*, 1980

VEGA

A thirst for green, because too long deprived
Of water in the stone garrigues, is natural,
Accumulates and then at last gets sated
By this lake which parodies a new life
With a boat outside the window, breathing:
Negative of a greater thirst no doubt,
Lying on slopes of water just multiplying

In green verdure, distributed at night
All on a dark floor, the sincere flavour of stars...

This we called Vega, a sly map-reference
Coded in telegrams the censored name to
'Vega next tenth of May. Okay?'
'Okay.' 'Okay.' You came.

The little train which joined then severed us
Clears Domodossola at night, doodles a way,
Tingling a single elementary bell,
Powdered with sequins of new snow,
To shamble at midnight into Stresa's blue.
One passenger only, a woman. You.

The fixed star of the ancients was another Vega,
A candle burning high in the alps of heaven,
Shielded by rosy fingers on some sill
Above some darkly sifted lake. They also knew
This silence trying to perfect itself in words.

Ah! The beautiful sail so unerringly on towards death
Once they experience the pith of this peerless calm.

Lawrence Durrell, from *Vega and Other Poems*, 1973

§

The movement of the train stimulates thought. Very few
people have been able to exploit this. I have heard it
rumoured that Rider Haggard, John Buchan, and John
Le Carré have all written books in trains, but I have been
able to find no hard evidence for this. As far as I know,
then, Trollope is the only author who has managed to
produce good literature while travelling on trains.

It was while I was engaged on *Barchester Towers* that I
adopted a system of writing which, for some years
afterwards, I found to be very serviceable to me. My
time was greatly occupied in travelling, and the nature

of my travelling was now changed. I could not any longer do it on horseback. Railroads afforded me my means of conveyance, and I found that I passed in railway-carriages very many hours of my existence. Like others, I used to read, – though Carlyle has since told me that a man when travelling should not read, but 'sit still and label his thoughts'. But if I intended to make a profitable business out of my writing, and, at the same time, to do my best for the Post Office, I must turn these hours to more account than I could do even by reading.

I made for myself therefore a little tablet, and found after a few days' exercise that I could write as quickly in a railway-carriage as I could at my desk. I worked with a pencil, and what I wrote my wife copied afterwards. In this way was composed the greater part of *Barchester Towers* and of the novel which succeeded it, and much also of others subsequent to them.

My only objection to the practice came from the appearance of literary ostentation, to which I felt myself to be subject when going to work before four or five fellow-passengers. But I got used to it. . .

Anthony Trollope, *An Autobiography*, 1883

WATERINGBURY TO BRICK. ARMS
FIRST CLASS
8 JAN. 20
352
PAID B £0.8.6

Browning apparently once found inspiration in the rhythm of the train. But, just as the old clickety-clack has been abolished by the introduction of continuously welded rails, so metrical poetry has given way to free verse.

A tune was born in my head last week,
 Out of the thump-thump and the shriek-shriek
Of the train, as I came by it, up from Manchester;
And when, next week, I take it back again,
My head will sing to the engine's clack again,
While it only makes my neighbour's haunches stir,
 – Finding no dormant musical sprout
In him, as in me, to be jolted out.

Robert Browning, from *Christmas-Eve and Easter-Day*, 1850

Graham Greene takes us a step further in considering why the train is such a good place for thinking. Maybe he should sue for copyright those big businesses which today inflict varieties of so-called 'white noise' on their personnel in an effort to aid concentration.

In the train, however fast it travelled, the passengers were compulsorily at rest; useless to try to follow any activity except of the mind; and that activity could be followed without fear of interruption. . . In the rushing reverberating express, noise was so regular that it was the equivalent of silence, movement was so continuous that after a while the mind accepted it as stillness.

Graham Greene, *Stamboul Train*, 1932

Henry Miller, one of the greatest and least understood writers of our time, provides another instance of loco-motive ratiocination. He also, incidentally, offers a clue as to why so few writers have followed Trollope's example. Deprive a modern author of his typewriter and he will be unable to write.

[63]

Clichy 1932

Going home in the train, I had a tremendous surge of ideas, caused by seeing the houses lit up in early evening; their bleak barren ugly qualities impressed me, and yet the soft light, often in a red-papered room, with people quietly sitting at the table, and coming in such quick succession – window after window – like souls exposed (where were the curtains . . . why hadn't the French used curtains ?), affected me strongly, affected me with the sense of drama, universes of drama in a short stretch between train stops. . . .

My mind surcharged on the train coming into Paris. Wanted to get home more quickly than I knew it possible, in order to write. . . Knew if I didn't go straight home I wouldn't write. . . Knowing that the mere act of getting off the train, the very stop of the train, the change of position, would burst the bubble. Fearing that greatly. Always the fear that one is not doing enough, that one is too indulgent with oneself, that the best thoughts are never written because they occur always when one cannot have access to the typewriter – and the question in my mind, is that so, or is that a weak man's defence ?

Henry Miller, *Letters to Anaïs Nin*, 1965

Most of us do not even think on trains, let alone write; we just vegetate. How well we understand and sympathize with Aldous Huxley's Denis and with no less a person than the Poet Laureate himself.

Oh, this journey ! It was two hours cut clean out of his life; two hours in which he might have done so much, so much – written the perfect poem, for example, or read the one illuminating book. Instead of which – his gorge rose at the smell of the dusty cushions against which he was leaning.

Two hours. One hundred and twenty minutes.

Anything might be done in that time. Anything. Nothing. Oh, he had had hundreds of hours, and what had he done with them? Wasted them, spilt the precious minutes as though his reservoir were inexhaustible. Denis groaned in the spirit, condemned himself utterly with all his works. What right had he to sit in the sunshine, to occupy corner seats in third-class carriages, to be alive? None, none, none.

Aldous Huxley, *Crome Yellow*, 1921

The old Great Western Railway shakes
The old Great Western Railway spins—
The old Great Western Railway makes
Me very sorry for my sins.

Sir John Betjeman, from *Distant View of a Provincial Town*, 1970

Hilaire Belloc did not read, or write, or think. He just went to sleep – and he felt no remorse either.

If the people of Milo did well to put up a statue in gold to the man that invented wheels, so should we also put one up in Portland stone or plaster to the man that invented rails, whose property it is not only to increase the speed and ease of travel, but also to bring on slumber as can no drug: not even poppies gathered under a waning moon.

Hilaire Belloc, *The Path to Rome*, 1902

Commuting

As well as offering occasional journeys in Nebraska, in the Balkans, in childhood, in the night, in the mind, the train, with complete impartiality, also provides what Professor Richard Cobb (who understands such matters) calls 'the regular urban itineraries of a respectable occupation'. Thus the train is for ever associated in many people's experience, not with the romantic and the unpredictable, but with 'the toad work' (Larkin).

This process of going to and fro and up and down, like Satan in the Book of Job, is known as commuting. The dictionaries allege that there used to be something called a commutation ticket and that the term derives from this. But those of us who make the daily journey to work by train know that commuting is so called because, over the years, it commutes or changes people from real human beings into programmed automata, into what Louis MacNeice describes as:

little sardine men crammed in a monster toy
Who tilt their aggregate beast against our crumbling
Troy.

Three prophetic utterances:

On all the line a sudden vengeance waits . . .
There passengers shall stand.

Alexander Pope, *Elegy to the Memory of an Unfortunate
Lady, c.* 1709

Alas, regardless of their doom,
The little victims play!
No sense have they of ills to come,
Nor care beyond today;

[66]

COMMUTING

Yet see how all around 'em wait
The Ministers of human fate,
    And black Misfortune's baleful train!

Thomas Gray, Ode on a Distant Prospect of Eton
College, 1742

Emprison'd in black, purgatorial rails.

John Keats, The Eve of St. Agnes, 1819

*'I had not thought death had undone so many', observes
T. S. Eliot (quoting Dante) in* The Waste Land *of the
morning commuters crossing London Bridge. E. B. White's
lines could be describing any one of them.*

COMMUTERS

Commuter – one who spends his life
In riding to and from his wife;
A man who shaves and takes a train
And then rides back to shave again.

E. B. White, from The Lady is Cold

*If Matthew Arnold's fellow-travellers were 'agitated',
this may well have been owing not to their fear of death,
but to their anxiety lest the old bore should choose to sit
in their compartment.*

At that time my avocations led me to travel almost
daily on one of the Great Eastern lines – the Woodford
Branch. . . The English middle class, of which I am
myself a feeble unit, travel on the Woodford Branch in
large numbers. . . Day after day I used to ply my
agitated fellow-travellers with all the consolations
which my transcendentalism, and my turn for the
French, would naturally suggest to me. . . I reminded
them what insignificant atoms we all are in the life of
the world. 'Suppose the worst to happen,' I said,
addressing a portly jeweller from Cheapside; 'suppose
even yourself to be the victim. . . We should miss you

for a day or two upon the Woodford Branch; but the great mundane movement would still go on; the gravel walks of your villa would still be rolled; dividends would still be paid at the Bank; omnibuses would still run; there would still be the old crush at the corner of Fenchurch Street.' All was of no avail. Nothing could moderate, in the bosom of the great English middle class, their passionate, absorbing, almost blood-thirsty clinging to life.

Matthew Arnold, *Preface to Essays in Criticism*, 1865

Matthew Arnold might receive short shrift from British Rail if he tried plying passengers with consolations today. But the man or woman who made the statement attributed to 'British Rail', in the last paragraph of this news item, deserves to be named and known. All too rarely do faceless spokespeople display such sensitivity.

THOU SHALT NOT PREACH, BR ORDAINS

A young woman who has been preaching the Gospel to commuters on suburban trains has been given a warning of possible prosecution for a breach of the peace from British Rail.

Miss Helen Dow, a veterinary student, aged 22, had been delivering sermons on early morning trains between Southport and Liverpool, where she is at university. When some passengers complained, a British Transport Police officer handed her an official warning, saying that she would be put off at the next stop if found preaching. If she continued to ignore warnings she might face prosecution.

Miss Dow did not preach on the trains yesterday. She said at her home at Waterloo, near Liverpool: 'At the moment I am praying for guidance.

'I started preaching on the trains some weeks ago.

This followed a dream in which I saw myself on a train giving God's message. I felt it was a revelation.'

British Rail said: 'No one doubts Miss Dow's sincerity, but people on trains often want to be quiet and go into worlds of their own.'

Guardian, 1 June 1978

Kenneth Grahame, author of The Wind in the Willows, *commuted to a job as Secretary of the Bank of England, and all the while longed to retire to the country.*

Our hour of sacrifice, alas, has not yet come. When it does – and may it be soon! – let the offering be no bloodless one, but let (for choice) a fat and succulent stationmaster smoke and crackle on the altar of expiation!

Kenneth Grahame, *Pagan Papers*, 1898

As in 1880, so in 1980. It is astonishing that, over the space of a century during which men have been to the moon and back, this particular scene has changed scarcely at all.

A dark torrent of human beings, chiefly men, gathered out of all the streets of the vicinity, had dashed unceasingly into the enclosure and covered the long platforms with trampling feet. Every few minutes a train rolled in, as if from some inexhaustible magazine of trains beyond the horizon, and, sucking into itself a multitude and departing again, left one platform for one moment empty, – and the next moment the platform was once more filled by the quenchless stream. Less frequently, but still often, other trains thundered through the station on a line removed from platforms, and these trains too were crammed with dark human beings, frowning in study over white newspapers. For even in 1880 the descent upon London from the suburbs was a formidable phenomenon. Train after train fled downwards with its freight towards the hidden city, and the torrent still surged, more rapid than ever, through the narrow gullet of the station. It was like the flight of some enormous and excited population from a country menaced with disaster.

Arnold Bennett, *Hilda Lessways*, 1911

And here is a rare poetic picture of those suburbs whence the short-haul commuters set out. In the short space of a sonnet the poet rises to the challenge of bringing out the beauty of the commonplace.

NEW CROSS
Suburban Landscape

Pallid with heat, a stark metallic sky
    Is looped above the siding, drably scarred
    With rails that flank a sooty engine-yard,
Ash-heaps and sheds and roofing all awry.

Derelict mouse-grey trucks are mirrored by
    The sepia of a mute canal, where charred
    Gasometers squat sullenly on guard,
And barges drowse and boilers faintly sigh.

To-night the arc-lamps, poised from slender stems,
    Will bloom like silvery fruits. Signals will gleam
With shifting specks of jade and crimson gems.

Then: music: hiss and gasp of throttled steam,
    Staccato gamut of the shunted trains,
    And murmurous diapason of the cranes.

Paul Selver, 1943

Even for those who manage, at weekends, to travel further afield than New Cross, on Monday mornings there is no escape.

COMMUTING

It is over. Now we sit
Reading the morning paper in the sound
Of the debilitating heavy train.
London again, again. London again.

Harold Monro, from *Week-End*

Who, in this Philip Larkin poem, are the dispossessed if not commuters? (Though I cannot understand why the platform is deserted. Perhaps, as it is 'darkening autumn', the poor man has forgotten to alter his watch at the end of Summer Time.) Larkin, of course, has written a train poem par excellence *in* The Whitsun Weddings *which proved, unfortunately, too long to include in its entirety and impossible to abridge without ruining 'the frail travelling coincidence'.*

One man walking a deserted platform;
Dawn coming, and rain
Driving across a darkening autumn;
One man restlessly waiting a train
While round the streets the wind runs wild,
Beating each shuttered house, that seems
Folded full of the dark silk of dreams,
A shell of sleep cradling a wife or child.

Who can this ambition trace,
To be each dawn perpetually journeying?
To trick this hour when lovers re-embrace
With the unguessed-at heart riding
The winds as gulls do? What lips said
Starset and cockcrow call the dispossessed
On to the next desert, lest
Love sink a grave round the still-sleeping head?

Philip Larkin, from *The North Ship*, 1945

Auden and Isherwood capture the essence of commuting in humdrum lines with a tedious rhythm.

No, nothing that matters will ever happen;
Nothing you'd want to put in a book;
Nothing to tell to impress your friends –
The old old story that never ends:
The eight o'clock train, the customary place,
Holding the paper in front of your face,
The public stairs, the glass swing-door,
The peg for your hat, the linoleum floor,
The office stool and the office jokes
And the fear in your ribs that slyly pokes:
Are they satisfied with you ?
Nothing interesting to do,
Nothing interesting to say,
Nothing remarkable in any way;
Then the journey home again
In the hot suburban train
To the tawdry new estate,
Crumpled, grubby, dazed and late:
Home to supper and to bed.
Shall we be like this when we are dead ?

W. H. Auden and Christopher Isherwood,
The Ascent of F. 6

*Commuting, no less than other areas of railway activity,
has its heroes and its martyrs. One such is stockbroker
Francis Dodgson.*

TAKING A TRAIN BY THE HORNS

BY GARETH PARRY

Bullfighting aficionados might, with profit, study the
work of Mr Francis Dodgson, at Manningtree, Essex,
station yesterday. To rousing cheers the 34-year-old
stockbroker stopped a snorting express dead in its
tracks and then rode all the way to Liverpool Street
with a victor's peremptory arrogance.

Mr Dodgson's deed arose from 'sheer frustration',
he said, after a two-hour meeting with British Rail
police officers who were waiting for him at Liverpool
Street.

'People had been waiting for a train for ages. I
realised the express would not stop unless I did
something about it. So I stepped on to the track and
stood there until it came to a halt a few feet away.'

Mr Dodgson, of Orvis Lane, East Bergholt, Suffolk,
had been waiting for his own commuter train for more
than an hour when he saw the 7.50 a.m. Hook of
Holland-Harwich boat train approaching Manningtree
station.

As it came through the junction at a careful 15 m.p.h.
Mr Dodgson swept on to the line carrying his bowler
hat and rolled umbrella. When the train stopped he
delivered a sharp lecture to the driver on punctuality,
and climbed into the first carriage.

British Rail said last night: 'The man's actions were
nothing short of lunacy.'

Guardian, 6 March 1975

*Thank goodness there is always humour – even if it is the
humour of the trenches.*

The pollen count was high, and Peter Cartwright had a violent fit of sneezing. He couldn't find a handkerchief, so he went round the corner of the 'gents', by the fire buckets, and blew his nose on the *Guardian*'s special Rhodesian supplement. He crumpled it up and put it in a green waste-paper basket.

'Sorry,' he said, rejoining Reggie. 'Ursula forgot my tissues.'

Reggie lent him his handkerchief. The eight-sixteen drew in five minutes late. Reggie stepped back as it approached for fear that he'd throw himself under the train. They managed to get seats. The rolling stock was nearing the end of its active life and Reggie was sitting over a wheel. The shaking caused his socks to fall down over his ankles, and it was hard to fill in the crossword legibly.

Shortly before Surbiton Peter Cartwright had another sneezing fit. He blew his nose on Reggie's handkerchief. It had 'R.I.P.' initialled on it.

'Finished,' said Peter Cartwright, pencilling in the last clue as they rattled through Raynes Park.

'I'm stuck on the top left-hand corner', said Reggie. 'I just don't know any Bolivian poets.'

The train arrived at Waterloo eleven minutes late. The loudspeaker announcement said that this was due to 'staff difficulties at Hampton Wick'.

David Nobbs, *The Fall and Rise of Reginald Perrin*, 1975

And this is something beyond humour, full of sympathy and humanity, arguably better observed than anything in The Great Railway Bazaar.

On that train, the 17.27 from Charing Cross, sat Ralph Gawber, an accountant. His thin face and his obvious fatigue gave him a look of kindliness, and he rode the train with tolerance, responding to the jump of the carriage with a gentle nod. In his heavy suit, in the harsh August heat, he had the undusted sanctity of a clergyman who has spent the day preaching without result in a stubborn slum. He held *The Times* in one hand, folded flat in a rectangle to make a surface for the crossword, and with the ball-point pen in his other hand he might have been studying a clue. But the crossword was completely inked in. Mr Gawber was asleep.

He had the elderly commuter's habit of being able to sleep without shifting position; sleep took him and embalmed him lightly like a touch of sadness he would soon shake off. He was dreaming of having tea with the Queen in a sunny room in Buckingham Palace. Jammed in the corner, the standing passengers' coats brushing his head, the lunchbox of the shirtless man next to him nudging his thigh, he dreamed. Around him, travellers slapped and shook their evening papers, but Mr Gawber slept on. The Queen suddenly smiled and leaned forwards and plucked open the front of her dress. Her full breasts tumbled out and Mr Gawber put his head between them and sobbed with shame and relief. They were so cool; and he felt her nipples against his ears.

Paul Theroux, *The Family Arsenal*, 1976

Not all dreamers are as privileged as Mr Gawber. As he sleeps, trains may catch the commuter unawares, conveying hints of his inadequacies.

Trains All that is vigorous and go-ahead in the dreamer.

His vitality and passions, his sexual mechanism. The individual's progress. 'Trains of thought'.

Missing the train: Fear of missing an opportunity, something critical; failing to make the progress he'd hoped for. There may no longer be enough energy to catch hold of life and make a success of it, or the

[75]

dreamer may be too anxious about getting ahead too fast and so spoil his chances, especially if he's been held back in the past.

Trying to get off the train : The dreamer is afraid of reaching his destination, afraid of an anticlimax; or perhaps the pace is too much for him.

Catching the train : An effort that has met with success. Ideally, after missing trains, the dreamer may start catching the trains later in the series of dreams, and later still may drive them.

The station : A woman; and the dreamer may draw up at the platform or hurtle through.

Arriving at a station : Death.

Tom Chetwynd, *Dictionary for Dreamers*, 1972

Graham Greene's Castle is a spy, a British intelligence officer working for the Russians. Book II of War and Peace *is for use as a code-book, not for reading. Otherwise Castle is just like any other middle-aged male commuter from Berkhamsted, whence Greene himself used to travel to MI6. Nobody knows how many spies commute. But every commuter knows the same feelings of guilt and insecurity as Castle.*

Castle left his bicycle with the ticket collector at Berkhamsted station and went upstairs to the London platform. He knew nearly all the commuters by sight – he was even on nodding terms with a few of them. A cold October mist was lying in the grassy pool of the castle and dripping from the willows into the canal on the other side of the line. He walked the length of the platform and back; he thought he recognised all the faces except for one woman in a shabby rabbity fur – women were rare on this train. He watched her climb into a compartment and he chose the same one so as to watch her more closely. The men opened newspapers and the woman opened a paper-bound novel by Denise

Robins. Castle began reading in Book II of *War and Peace*. It was a breach of security, even a small act of defiance, to read this book publicly for pleasure.

Graham Greene, *The Human Factor*, 1978,

Donald Maclean was a real life commuting spy. I have always loved the assumption of the MI5 surveillance team that, once a commuter has boarded his regular train, there is nowhere he can go but home. In fact Maclean realized every commuter's dream and proved that, providing you have sufficient breadth of vision, the 5.19 from Charing Cross can take you anywhere in the world. And to give MI5 their due, they too may have been well aware of this.

After luncheon Maclean went to the Travellers', cashed a cheque for five pounds – a small sum for a man considering a journey – and after a couple of scotches at the comfortable downstairs bar at the back of the building returned to his desk in the American Department. At 5.19, as usual on his good days, he boarded the train from Charing Cross to Sevenoaks. The MI5 contingent followed him conscientiously as far as the barrier, and there they stopped. They had no orders to continue beyond this point. For some reason MI5 had assumed that he could not come to any harm in the pastoral suburban scene of Tatsfield.

Bruce Page, David Leitch, Philip Knightley,
The Philby Conspiracy

Concluding this section, Richard Jefferies offers a ray of mystical hope to all commuters, whatever the nationality of the grain-harvest on which they depend.

Another train booms across the iron bridge in the hollow. In a few hours now the carriages will be crowded with men hastening home from their toil in the City. The narrow streak of sunshine which day by day falls for a little while upon the office floor, yellowed by the dingy pane, is all, perhaps, to remind them of the sun and sky, of the forces of nature; and that little is unnoticed. The pressure of business is so severe in these later days that in the hurry and excitement it is not wonderful many should forget that the world is not comprised in the court of a City thoroughfare.

Rapt and absorbed in discount and dollars, in bills and merchandise, the over-strung mind deems itself all – the body is forgotten, the physical body, which is subject to growth and change, just as the plants and the very grass of the field. But there is a subtle connection between the physical man and the great nature which comes pressing up so closely to the metropolis. He still depends in the nineteenth century, as in the dim ages before the Pyramids, upon this tiny yellow grain here, rubbed out from the ear of wheat. The clever mechanism of the locomotive which bears him to and fro, week after week and month after month, from home to office and from office home, has not rendered him in the least degree independent of this.

Richard Jefferies, *Wheatfields*, 1893

Mixed Goods

The variety of uses to which trains can be put and the variety of inspiration which they can provide are limitless.

A railway isn't just carriages and a locomotive and a permanent way. It's a sort of door. At any time you can open it and take to the road, turning your back on a home that's dreary and on a life that's a misery to you. Any time you fancy you can whizz off to a new home and a new life, in any place you choose. Whenever you're down in the dumps – just open the door.

Clifford Dyment, *The Railway Game*, 1962

I doubt whether Dickens's Mr Carker, the traveller in the next piece, would have agreed with Clifford Dyment. He was plainly suffering from the forerunner of jet-lag or circadian dysrhythmia.

'What day is this?' he asked of the waiter, who was making preparations for his dinner.

'Day, Sir?'

'Is it Wednesday?'

'Wednesday, Sir? No, Sir. Thursday, Sir.'

'I forgot. How goes the time? My watch is unwound.'

'Wants a few minutes of five o'clock, Sir. Been travelling a long time, Sir, perhaps?'

'Yes.'

'By rail, Sir?'

'Yes.'

'Very confusing, Sir. Not much in the habit of travelling by rail myself, Sir, but gentlemen frequently say so.'

Charles Dickens, *Dombey and Son*, 1846–8

Mr Carker might have been less confused if he had had access to a copy of Bradshaw's Railway Guide, *the legendary timetable published continuously from 1839 until as recently as 1961. On the other hand, he might not, for the* Guide *was notoriously difficult to decipher.*

Zuleika Dobson had her own way of solving the problem.

... and now she wheeled round and swiftly glided to that little table on which stood her two books. She snatched Bradshaw.

We always intervene between Bradshaw and anyone whom we see consulting him. 'Mademoiselle will

---

No. I.   *6th Mo. (JUNE), 1847.*

BRADSHAW'S
CONTINENTAL RAILWAY,
STEAM NAVIGATION, & CONVEYANCE

AND TRAVELLER'S MANUAL

FOR THE

WHOLE CONTINENT OF EUROPE:

CONTAINING EVERY INFORMATION CONNECTED WITH RAILWAYS, STEAM NAVIGATION, AND CONVEYANCES;

AND PRACTICAL INSTRUCTIONS FOR TRAVELLERS.

PRICE ONE SHILLING,
ACCOMPANIED WITH A WELL EXECUTED MAP OF THE RAILWAYS

PARIS.

PUBLISHED BY GALLIGNANI & Co., 18, RUE VIVIENNE; W. C. BERNARDY, 13, CITE VINDE, BOULT DE LA MADELEINE;

BRUSSELS:—W. MIDDLETON, 92, MONTAGNE DE LA COUR.

LONDON:—Published at BRADSHAW'S GENERAL RAILWAY PUBLICATION OFFICE, 59, FLEET-STREET;—W. J. ADAMS, AGENT.

MANCHESTER:—BRADSHAW AND BLACKLOCK, 27, BROWN-STREET.

BRADSHAW AND BLACKLOCK, PRINTERS.

---

permit me to find that which she seeks?' asked
Mélisande.

'Be quiet,' said Zuleika. We always repulse, at first,
anyone who intervenes between us and Bradshaw.

We always end by accepting the intervention. 'See if
it is possible to go direct from here to Cambridge,' said
Zuleika, handing the book on. 'If it isn't, then – well,
see how one *does* get there.'

We never have any confidence in the intervener. Nor
is the intervener, when it comes to the point, sanguine.
With mistrust mounting to exasperation Zuleika sat
watching the faint and frantic researches of her maid.

'Stop!' she said suddenly. 'I have a much better
idea. Go down very early to the station. See the
stationmaster. Order me a special train. For ten o'clock,
say.'

Max Beerbohm, *Zuleika Dobson*, 1911

*Arnold Bennett and P. G. Wodehouse show their charac-
ters rising to the challenge, and even finding poetry in the
intricacies of Bradshaw.*

Harry set himself to one of his favourite studies –
Bradshaw. He always handled Bradshaw like a master,
accomplishing feats of interpretation that amazed his
wife.

Arnold Bennett, *These Twain*, 1916

Come, Angela, let us read together in a book more
moving than the Koran, more eloquent than Shakes-
peare, the book of books, the crown of all literature –
Bradshaw's Railway Guide.

P. G. Wodehouse, *Meet Mr Mulliner*, 1927

*Mr Slope, hypocritical and scheming chaplain to Bishop
Proudie, had his own devious reasons for studying
Bradshaw. However, many more pleasant Victorians than
Mr Slope disapproved of train travel on Sundays.*

'I fear there is a great deal of Sabbath travelling here,' said Mr Slope. 'On looking at the "Bradshaw", I see that there are three trains in and three out every Sabbath. Could nothing be done to induce the company to withdraw them? Don't you think, Dr Grantly, that a little energy might diminish the evil?'

'Not being a director, I really can't say. But if you can withdraw the passengers, the company, I dare say, will withdraw the trains', said the doctor. 'It's merely a question of dividends.'

Anthony Trollope, *Barchester Towers*, 1857

§

Troop trains did not find their way into Bradshaw. They belonged to another world which was at the same time unreal and yet all too real. What I find striking is the new perspective gained by contemplating 'The Send-Off' not as a war poem but as a train poem.

THE SEND-OFF

Down the close, darkening lanes they sang their way
To the siding-shed,
And lined the train with faces grimly gay.

Their breasts were stuck all white with wreath and
      spray
As men's are, dead.

Dull porters watched them, and a casual tramp
Stood staring hard,
Sorry to miss them from the upland camp.
Then, unmoved, signals nodded, and a lamp
Winked to the guard.

So secretly, like wrongs hushed-up, they went.
They were not ours:
We never heard to which front these were sent.

Nor there if they yet mock what women meant
Who gave them flowers.

Shall they return to beatings of great bells
In wild train-loads ?
A few, a few, too few for drums and yells,
May creep back, silent, to still village wells
Up half-known roads.

Wilfred Owen

*Captain Owen Rutter's troop train (from Taranto to Le
Havre) is more jolly than Wilfred Owen's. This is not
only – if at all – because Owen's men are privates and
Rutter's are officers. It is a question of the humour which
Owen, for all his moving poetry, notably lacks.*

> Tiadatha'd learnt the lesson
> Which is learnt by every traveller,
> That wherever you may wander
> You should never be uncomfy
> Any longer than you've got to.

The Song of Tiadatha *is a beautiful long poem in the
metre of Longfellow's* Hiawatha – *much more than just a
parody – telling the story of Tiadatha's (equals Tired
Arthur) war experiences mainly in Greece.*

> Very wisely Tiadatha
> And his friend the gunner captain
> Went and bagged a carriage early,
> Went and bagged a first-class carriage
> That had still some cushions in it
> And some glass left in the windows,
> Chalked up 'Captain Tiadatha
> And three officers' upon it,
> Got two merchants who were going
> One night only on the journey,
> After which they shared the carriage
> Tiadatha and the gunner.

Early every day they halted,
Washed in buckets by the trainside,
Shaved and strolled about a little,
Sometimes snatched a hurried breakfast
At the buffet of a station.
Spent the long, long days in reading,
Pulling mutual friends to pieces,
Talking over raids and battles,
Talking over all their leave plans,
Ate their very sketchy luncheons,
Ate their very uncouth dinners,
Cleaned their plates with bits of paper,
Cleaned their knives and forks with paper,
Living in acute discomfort,
Pigging as they'd seldom pigged it,
Turning out sometimes at Rest Camps
Just to stretch their legs a little,
Have a bath and get some dinner.
Every night they got a fug up,
Got a most uncommon fug up,
Boarded up the broken windows,
Lighted quite a dozen candles.
All along the rack they stuck them,
Stuck them on the greasy arm-rests,
Got the carriage warm and cosy,
Then unrolled their fat valises,
Slept beneath a pile of blankets
Soundly as a pair of kittens.
Thus nine days and nights they travelled. . .

Owen Rutter, *The Song of Tiadatha*, 1919

Another breed who have little need of timetables are the hoboes or tramps who hitch free rides on trains, often at risk to life and limb. The Welsh writer W. H. Davies, who spent some years bumming around America before he lost a leg trying to jump a freight train, explains the technique.

I was soon initiated into the mysteries of beating my way by train, which is so necessary in parts of that country [USA], seeing the great distances between towns. Sometimes we were fortunate enough to get an empty car; sometimes we had to ride the bumpers; and often, when travelling through a hostile country, we rode on the roof of a car, so as not to give the brakesman an opportunity of striking us off the bumpers unawares. It is nothing unusual in some parts to find a man, always a stranger, lying dead on the track, often cut in many pieces. At the inquest they invariably bring in a verdict of accidental death, but we know different. Therefore we rode the car's top, so as to be at no disadvantage in a struggle. The brakesman, knowing well that our fall would be his own, would not be too eager to commence hostilities.

Sometimes we were desperate enough to ride the narrow iron rods, which were under the car, and only a few feet from the track. This required some nerve, for it was not only uncomfortable, but the train, being so near the line, seemed to be running at a reckless and uncontrollable speed, whereas, when riding on the car's top, a much faster train seems to be running much slower and far more smooth and safe. Sometimes we were forced to jump off a moving train at the point of a revolver. At other times the brakesmen were friendly, and even offered assistance in the way of food, drink or tobacco. Again, when no firearm was in evidence, we had to threaten the brakesman with death if he interfered with us. In this way Brum and myself travelled the States of America, sleeping at night by camp fires, and taking temporary possession of empty houses.

W. H. Davies, *The Autobiography of a Super-Tramp*, 1907

THE TRAIN

The American Hart Crane gives a more poetic picture of the hoboes.

                                             Behind
My father's cannery works I used to see
Rail-squatters ranged in nomad raillery,
The ancient men – wifeless or runaway
Hobo-trekkers that forever search
An empire wilderness of freight and rails.
Each seemed a child, like me, on a loose perch,
Holding to childhood like some termless play.
John, Jake or Charley, hopping the slow freight
– Memphis to Tallahassee – riding the rods,
Blind fists of nothing, humpty-dumpty clods.

Hart Crane, The River, April 1930

Who more sincerely than a hobo could sing:

> 'This life so free
> Is the thing for me'?

Trust Thomas Hardy to invest the words with the deepest irony by putting them into the mouth of a convict.

AT THE RAILWAY STATION, UPWAY

'There is not much that I can do,
    For I've no money that's quite my own!'
  Spoke up the pitying child –
A little boy with a violin
At the station before the train came in, –
'But I can play my fiddle to you,
And a nice one 'tis, and good in tone!'

The man in the handcuffs smiled;
The constable looked, and he smiled, too,
    As the fiddle began to twang;
And the man in the handcuffs suddenly sang
        With grimful glee:
        'This life so free
        Is the thing for me!'

And the constable smiled, and said no word,
As if unconscious of what he heard;
And so they went on till the train came in –
The convict, and boy with the violin.

Thomas Hardy

*Poor Oscar Wilde had no small boy with a violin to play
to him at Clapham Junction.*

On November 13th 1895 I was brought down here
from London. From two o'clock till half-past two on
that day I had to stand on the centre platform of
Clapham Junction in convict dress and handcuffed,
for the world to look at. I had been taken out of the
Hospital Ward without a moment's notice being given
to me. Of all possible objects I was the most grotesque.
When people saw me they laughed. Each train as it
came up swelled the audience. Nothing could exceed
their amusement. That was of course before they knew
who I was. As soon as they had been informed, they
laughed still more. For half an hour I stood there in the
grey November rain surrounded by a jeering mob.

Oscar Wilde, letter to Lord Alfred Douglas, parts of
which were published as *De Profundis*, written in
HM Prison, Reading, early 1897

*Although Oscar Wilde must at some stage have stood on
Reading platform, D. H. Lawrence is probably imper-
fectly remembering the Clapham Junction incident here.
His* Sea and Sardinia *(1923) is full of good writing about
trains.*

Two convicts chained together among the crowd – and
two soldiers. The prisoners wear fawny homespun
clothes, of cloth such as the peasants weave, with
irregularly occurring brown stripes. Rather nice
handmade rough stuff. But linked together, dear God!
And those horrid caps on their hairless foreheads. No

hair. Probably they are going to a convict station on the Lipari islands. The people take no notice. . .

Standing on Messina station – dreary, dreary hole – and watching the winter rain and seeing the pair of convicts, I must remember again Oscar Wilde on Reading platform, a convict.

And still today escorted prisoners mingle from time to time with ordinary passengers on regular services.

Unexplained delay at Didcot. (Nothing abnormal about that.) At last two uniformed soldiers board train. Handcuffed to one of them a pugnacious looking, close-cropped, bedenimed youth. Train moves off. Law-abiding commuters look variously annoyed, smug, curious, compassionate, indifferent. We should not. And therefore never send to know. Casual travellers do not notice our handcuffs. Few of us sense the bracelets round our own wrists. But they are there, along with the uniformed escort. Man is born free and is everywhere in trains.

Roger Green, *A Commuter's Notebook*

One who managed not to end up behind bars was E. V. Knox's Percy. John Masefield had published in 1911 The Everlasting Mercy, *a long poetic account of how a hardened criminal repented and reformed. But you do not have to know the original to enjoy the parody.*

from THE EVERLASTING PERCY
or *Masefield on the Railway Centenary*

> For several years I was so wicked
> I used to go without a ticket,
> And travelled underneath the seat
> Down in the dust of people's feet,
> Or else I sat as bold as brass
> And told them 'Season' in first class.
> In 1921, at Harwich,
> I smoked in a non-smoking carriage;
> I never knew what Life or Art meant,
> I wrote 'Reserved' on my compartment,
> And once (I was a guilty man)
> I swapped the labels in guard's van.
> From 1922 to 4
> I leant against the carriage door
> Without a-looking at the latch;
> And once, a-leaving Colney Hatch,
> I put a huge and heavy parcel
> Which I were taking to Newcastle,
> Entirely filled with lumps of lead,
> Up on the rack above my head;
> And when it tumbled down, oh Lord!
> I pulled communication cord.
> The guard came round and said, 'You mule!
> What have you done, you dirty fool?'
> I simply sat and smiled, and said
> 'Is this train right for Holyhead?'
> He said 'You blinking blasted swine,
> You'll have to pay the five-pound fine'.

I gave a false name and address,
Puffed up with my vaingloriousness.
At Bickershaw and Strood and Staines
I've often got on moving trains,
And once alit at Norwood West
Before my coach had come to rest.
A window and a lamp I broke
At Chipping Sodbury and Stoke
And worse I did at Wissendine:
I threw out bottles on the line
And other articles as be
Likely to cause great injury
To persons working on the line –
That's what I did at Wissendine.
I grew so careless what I'd do
Throwing things out, and dangerous too,
That, last and worst of all I'd done,
I threw a great sultana bun
Out of the train at Pontypridd –
It hit a platelayer, it did.
I thought that I should have to swing
And never hear the sweet birds sing.
The jury recommended mercy,
And that's how grace was given to Percy.

E. V. Knox

*The Chairman of the Bench of Magistrates most certainly
did not recommend mercy for Mr Toad of Toad Hall. He
sent him down for twenty years for motoring offences and
rudeness to the police. But Toad made his escape and,
with the help of a sympathetic engine-driver, eluded the
hue and cry following on another locomotive.*

They piled on more coals, and the train shot into the
tunnel, and the engine rushed and roared and rattled,
till at last they shot out at the other end into fresh air
and the peaceful moonlight, and saw the wood lying

dark and helpful upon either side of the line. The driver
shut off steam and put on brakes, the Toad got down on
the step, and as the train slowed down to almost a
walking pace he heard the driver call out, 'Now, jump!'

Toad jumped, rolled down a short embankment,
picked himself up unhurt, scrambled into the wood
and hid.

Peeping out, he saw his train get up speed again and
disappear at a great pace. Then out of the tunnel
burst the pursuing engine, roaring and whistling, her
motley crew waving their various weapons and shout-
ing, 'Stop! stop! stop!' When they were past, the Toad
had a hearty laugh – for the first time since he was
thrown into prison.

Kenneth Grahame, *The Wind in the Willows*, 1908

*Quite as delinquent as Toad and equally impenitent are
the Revd. W. Awdry's trucks. Awdry has written dozens
of railway books for children. The best known are probably
those featuring the likeable, cheerful tank-engine Thomas.
But read all the books carefully and you will find yourself
in a sadistic, discriminatory world where all engines are
good, and all trucks are bad and to be smashed to pieces if
they disobey.*

When Oliver came home again, the trucks sang rude
songs. They were led by Scruffey, a 'Private Owner'
wagon. . .

The engines bumped them. 'Shut up!' they ordered.
But they couldn't be everywhere; and everywhere they
weren't, the trucks began again. . .

Oliver marshalled the worst trucks two by two in
front of Toad.

'This way, Mr Oliver, takes longer, but they can't
give trouble, and if you leave that Scruffey till last,
you'll have him behind you. Then you can bump him
if he starts his nonsense.'. . .

'Hold back!' whispered Scruffey. The trucks giggled as they passed the word.

Oliver dug his wheels into the sand, and gave a mighty heave.

'Ooer!' groaned Scruffey. His couplings tightened. He was stretched between Oliver and the trucks. 'I don't like this!'

'Go it!' yelled Duck. 'Well done, Boy, WELL DONE!'

'Ow! Ow!' wailed Scruffey, but no one bothered about him. 'Ow! Ooooow! I'm coming apaaaaaart!'

There came a rending, splitting crash.

Oliver shot forward suddenly. Scruffey's front end bumped behind his bunker, while Scruffey's load spread itself over the track.

'Well, Oliver, so you don't know your own strength! Is that it?'

'N-n-no, Sir,' said Oliver nervously.

The Fat Controller inspected the remains.

'As I thought,' he remarked. 'Rotten wood, rusty frames – unserviceable before it came.' He winked at Oliver, and whispered, 'Don't tell the trucks that – bad for discipline!'

He strode away, chuckling.

Nowadays, Oliver only takes trucks when the other engines are busy; but they always behave well. 'Take care with Mr Oliver,' they warn each other. 'He's strong he is. You play tricks on him, and he'll likely pull you in half.'

Revd. W. Awdry, *Oliver the Western Engine*, 1969

Charles Lutwidge Dodgson (any relation, I wonder, to Francis Dodgson of Essex?), alias Lewis Carroll, used, whenever he travelled by train, to carry with him a complete kit of puzzles, games, toys, riddles, to assist him in chatting up small girls.

IN A RAILWAY COMPARTMENT

Oxford to London, 1884:
Against the crimson arm-rest leaned a girl
Drumming her heels in boredom on the floor
Until a white-haired gentleman who saw
She hated travelling produced a case
Of puzzles: 'Seven Germans run a race...
Unwind this maze, escape the lion's paw...
The princess must be lowered by her hair...'
The train entered a tunnel, shrieking, all
The lights went out and when he took her hand
She was the princess in the tower and
A lion faced her on the moonlit wall
Who roared and reached and caught and held her there.

John Fuller, from *Fairground Music* 1961

*This is how Lewis Carroll transmuted such experiences
into a fiction that was surreal before its time.*

'Tickets, please!' said the Guard, putting his head in
at the window. In a moment everybody was holding
out a ticket: they were about the same size as the people,
and quite seemed to fill the carriage.

'Now then! Show your ticket, child!' the Guard
went on, looking angrily at Alice. And a great many
voices all said together ('like the chorus of a song,'
thought Alice), 'Don't keep him waiting, child! Why,
his time is worth a thousand pounds a minute!'

'I'm afraid I haven't got one,' Alice said in a fright-
ened tone: 'there wasn't a ticket-office where I came
from.' And again the chorus of voices went on. 'There
wasn't room for one where she came from. The land
there is worth a thousand pounds an inch!'

'Don't make excuses,' said the Guard: 'you should
have bought one from the engine-driver.' And once
more the chorus of voices went on with 'The man that

drives the engine. Why, the smoke alone is worth a thousand pounds a puff!'

Lewis Carroll, *Through the Looking-Glass and What Alice Found There*, 1871

But in case we should think that the idea of the guard 'putting his head in at the window' is purely imaginary, Patrick Leigh Fermor travelling in Greece in the 1950s, delightfully corrects us.

The carriage that bore us along a narrow-gauge track seemed obsolete as an equipage in a museum. High and narrow, the coachwork was painted to mimic the graining of yellow wood and upholstered in threadbare tasselled velvet. This delightful carriage, fit for two travellers out of Jules Verne, carried us swaying through the Thracian sky and over the gorges and forests of plane trees, the rocky river beds and the scrub-mantled mountainsides at an abnormal height. The ancient Thracians used to hold their mares with their heads downwind in order that the wind might put them in foal. Over which of the Rhodope passes did this invisible stallion come snorting ? . . .

As though its owner were flying alongside, a jovial, unshaven face appeared in the tall frame of the window. It was the ticket collector. When he had climbed in and pocketed our tickets, we watched him work his perilous way along the duckboard of the corridorless train like a cat-burglar.

Patrick Leigh Fermor, *Roumeli*, 1966

The surreal sublime, as far as trains are concerned, must be Edward Upward's The Railway Accident. *Since that long story is a seamless garment, quite unbiodegradable, this snatch of Auden, written under the influence of his friend Upward, must suffice.*

The nine o'clock business train leaves on a mystery trip through the more remote upland valleys; there is no refreshment car. Packed excursions at five-minute intervals, jumping the points, enter the sea from Craigendoran Pier.

W. H. Auden, *The Orators*, 1932

From the surreal to... what? Maybe one day somebody will write a thesis demonstrating that the place of J.R.R. Tolkien, author of The Hobbit *and* The Lord of the Rings, *is among the thriller-writers. Meanwhile it is revealing to note that he shared with Ian Fleming a fascination with the legends on the sides of rolling-stock. Tolkien's interest began when, as a child, he lived at King's Heath near Birmingham.*

The King's Heath house backed on to a railway line, and life was punctuated by the roar of trains and the shunting of trucks in the nearby coal-yard. Yet the railway cutting had grass slopes, and here he discovered flowers and plants. And something else attracted his attention: the curious names on the coal-trucks in the sidings below, odd names which he did not know how to pronounce but which had a strange appeal to him. So it came about that by pondering over *Nantyglo, Senghenydd, Blaen-Rhondda, Penrhiwceiber,* and *Trede-gar,* he discovered the existence of the Welsh language.

Humphrey Carpenter, *J. R. R. Tolkien, a Biography*, 1977

To my great regret I have not managed to unearth anything on the extraordinary names bestowed (by whom?) on the trucks themselves – Crocodile, Macaw, Weltrol, Boplate, Dogfish, Mermaid and the rest.

Bond turned to the window and watched the pretty clap-board houses slip by as they approached Trenton. He loved trains and he looked forward with excitement to the rest of the journey.

The train was slowing down. They slid past sidings full of empty freight cars bearing names from all over the States – 'Lackawanna', 'Chesapeke and Ohio', 'Lehigh Valley', 'Seaboard Fruit Express', and the lilting 'Acheson, Topeka and Santa Fé' – names that held all the romance of the American railroads.

'British Railways ?' thought Bond. He sighed and turned his thoughts back to the present adventure.

Ian Fleming, *Live And Let Die*, 1954

The poet Louis MacNeice, in his autobiography, finds the names on the trucks somehow symbolic of the decline of England.

In the summer of 1927 we used to paddle our canoe along the evil-smelling canal through the slums or up the Isis past the gas-drums. One May morning we were on this stretch of the Isis watching a dragonfly among the cow-parsley and shards on the bank when a goods train came over the railway bridge and we made a chant out of the names on the trucks – Hickleton, Hickleton, Hickleton, Lunt, Hickleton, Longbotham. This incantation of names at once became vastly symbolic – symbolic of an idle world, of oily sunlit water and willows and willows' reflections and, mingled with the idleness, a sense of things worn out, scrap-iron and refuse, the shadow of the gas-drum, this England. Hickleton Hickleton Hickleton – the long train clanked and rumbled as if it had endless time to reach wherever it was going. The placid dotage of a great industrial country.

Louis MacNeice, *The Strings Are False*, 1965

Kenneth Ashley goes even further. To him the names, and the trucks themselves, speak of life, hope, love. We have moved a long way from the Reverend W. Awdry and poor Scruffey torn apart for his disobedience.

[96]

The station is empty and desolate;
A sick lamp wanly glows;
Slowly puffs a goods engine,
Slow yet alive with great energy;
Drawing rumbling truck
After rumbling, rumbling truck;
Big, half-seen, insensate.
Yet each as it jolts through the glow
Responds to the questioning light
Dumbly revealing
Diverse personality:
'Neal & Co.'; 'John Bugsworth'; 'Norland
    Collieries Limited';
'Jolly & Sons'; 'Jolly & Sons'; 'Jolly & Sons';
Thrice repeated, percussive, insistent –
Each wet wall-side successively announcing
Names: badges and symbols of men,
Of men in their intricate trafficking –
But there quickens a deeper emotion,
Roused by the iterant names,
Beyond the mere intricate commerce,
The infinite wonder of life.
Effort and hope and love, the heart's desire,
Leap in the womb of the brain
As the trucks clang their way through the night.

From *Goods Train at Night*

§

Despite the conservationist misgivings of Wordsworth and others, the railways, with their secluded cuttings and embankments, have actually benefited flora and fauna. All the more so now that more and more lines are lapsing into a tranquillity undisturbed by trains.

Beyond the river Yantle we come upon a line of railway, running down from Chipping Norton to join the main line to Worcester... The main railway is here joined by two subsidiary lines, the one coming from Chipping Norton and the other from Cheltenham over the Cotswolds. Paradoxical as it may seem, I do not hesitate to say that this large mileage of railway within a small radius acts beneficially upon our bird-life.

W. Warde Fowler, *A Year with the Birds*, 1889

Perhaps the most famous railway plant is Oxford ragwort. This came originally from the slopes of Etna and Vesuvius. It escaped from the Oxford Botanic Garden on to some walls in Oxford. By 1830 it had spread into adjacent villages. As soon as the Great Western line was opened it spread along the tracks, and its seed drifted in and out of the carriages, as the passengers entered and left.

From an article, 'Once the Trains Have Gone: Wildlife of Railway Lines', by Richard Gulliver. *Country Life*, 31 January 1980

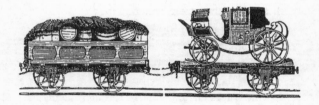

The Permanent Way?

In a pamphlet published by British Rail to mark the 125th anniversary of Paddington Station in 1979, somebody wrote:

The smoke, noise and colour of the bygone steam age have given way to the sleek and effortless efficiency of the high speed era. What, one wonders, would Brunel have made of the present?

Without pausing to consider the enormous begged question in the first sentence, without daring to suggest answers to the rash inquiry in the second, I cannot help wondering what the great Victorian engineer would have thought of the future. The crystal ball is clouded, but it certainly looks as though, after 150 years, the end of the line is near. When children withdraw their support from something, that is always an ominous sign. They used to wait in fields and wave at passing trains; now they stand on railway bridges and heave bricks at them.

Let us begin this last section as we began the first, with Dombey and Son. *Here ends Dickens's working and development of the railway theme in this novel. It is a tour de force from the arrival of the railway, through its general impact, then its specific influence on the very speech of an individual, its potential as a metaphor for death, its disruption of time, to, finally, its ability to inflict death. ('He' is James Carker, the villain of the piece.)*

He was walking to and fro, alone, looking along the lines of iron, across the valley in one direction, and towards a dark bridge near at hand in the other; when, turning in his walk, where it was bounded by one end of the wooden stage on which he paced up and down, he saw the man from whom he had fled, emerging from the door by which he himself had entered there. And their eyes met.

In the quick unsteadiness of the surprise, he staggered, and slipped on to the road below him. But recovering his feet immediately, he stepped back a pace or two upon that road, to interpose some wider space between them, and looked at his pursuer, breathing short and quick.

He heard a shout – another – saw the face change from its vindictive passion to a faint sickness and terror – felt the earth tremble – knew in a moment that the rush was come – uttered a shriek – looked round – saw the red eyes, bleared and dim, in the daylight, close upon him – was beaten down, caught up, and whirled away upon a jagged mill, that spun him round and round, and struck him limb from limb, and licked his stream of life up with its fiery heat, and cast his mutilated fragments in the air.

Dickens was able to use the train as a convenient device for disposing of his villain. Real life, of course, is far more capricious, as Robert Service points out.

THE DISASTER

Said Vi: 'My dear, you'll miss your train.
   It's nearly eight, you ought to hurry.'
I took the short cut by the lane,
   In pea-soup fog the trees were blurry.
And when I reached the wicket gate,
   The station clock was pointing eight.

My train was slowly pulling out.
   'You'll have to run,' the porter said.
I could have made it, I've no doubt;
   I sprinted. . . then I shrieked with dread:

I saw my coach upend and smash,
  Then others pile with crash and crash.

Aye, with those eyes I saw it plain,
  The North Express come roaring through,
To telescope our local train,
  And rear in hideous wreckage too:
With devil's din and cloud of steam,
  And crumpled cars, and scream – and scream.

Over a hundred were the dead;
  But what of those who did not die!
I strove to them with hands that bled,
  'Mid twisted steel I saw them lie:
The raving ones who begged in vain
  For morphine to relieve their pain.

"'Tis Providence you're safe,' said Vi.
  Said I: 'Oh Providence my hat!
If He knew what would happen, why
  Could He not have prevented that?
Or did He give no sign because
  He could not override His Laws?'

Robert Service

§

This anthology demonstrates nothing more clearly than the strange power of the train to generate thought, especially thought about huge abstracts like life, death, religion, destiny (oddly, not, on the whole, love). Here the writer is reviewing a play whose entire action takes place on a train (Prisoner and Escort *by Charles Wood*).

For the truth is that the train, and by extension the whole material universe of which it is part, cares nothing for the people in it. . . Whether the men are quarrelling or quiescent, the train roars indifferently on. The lights of passed stations glimmer for a moment, the darkness of the night is split as by an arrow, and nothing that men do or think alters by an iota the headlong journey.

Harold Hobson, in the *Sunday Times*, 6 July 1975

A depressing railway journey by night seems to have led Frances Cornford to conclude that fate is not just indifferent, but actively hostile. Anyone who has ever been marooned on Didcot station in the small hours will know the feeling.

FIGURES ON THE PLATFORM

Travelling at night no man has any home
Beyond the station's melancholy dome.
The giant tired engine starts again
For homeless fields anonymous in rain,
Now it has gone. But that was not our train.
Even the kit-bag and the trundled can
Are cared-for and considered more than man
Who has been travelling since his life began.

His soul, uncomforted by cups of tea,
Envies the soul of the baby on his knee,
Escaped in peace from its small house of sense.
Even his grin for the barmaid was pretence;
And soon his cup will lose its tiny heat
Abandoned on the desert of a seat;
Even the bottom sip was hardly sweet
And held no hope; it tasted sad, of spoon.

O, if our journey's end were coming soon,
But will it ever come in a thousand hours?
We are the prey of adamantine powers,
Remote, uncaring, cold, yet easily crossed;
They may not punish us for being lost
If we remain their puppets, twitched and tossed,
They may not quite malevolently mind
Our presence here, if hopelessly resigned.

Frances Cornford

*The train makes us think of our mortality, but its own days
are numbered too. Steam trains have gone. The others will
follow. Giving them spurious titles like 'High Speed' and
'Advanced' will not save them.*

THE LAST TRAIN

Suddenly awake at two, and aware of the disintegration
Of silence by the distant but steadily growing louder
Travelling of a multitude of metal, a remnant of a
    regiment
Of defeated men in armour overweighted by retreat,
Without hope, late, lost, but continuing all along
In the habitual rhythm of discipline, of one last order
    obeyed.

That's what it is! Of course it is the last, the very last
Train; they said it would go past tonight, the long
Last train of all, before the closing of the line.
Under a clear chill moon, loud now but growing no
    louder
In clattering concatenation it goes reverberating on
Unhurried, and clanking already, already, a little less
    loud.

They make it give out a long clear whistle, a thrilling
Scream as of some rare owl when huge-eyed at knowing
Itself last of all its kind its utterance is despair;
It is a brontosaurus lumbering off into the ultimate
Exile of solitude, without mate or progeny, unadap-
    table,
Wielding in a laborious gait its huge unwanted limbs.

Extinction is signalled. This is the end of the Age of
    Steam
(Like all others a devouring age) and with it one more
Realized fantasy of power has receded into history;

The ancestral pistons seem like playthings now, the
    linked-up
Old iron trucks and bogied cars of this last trundling
    train
And their knocking rhythm dwindling along the
    impermanent way.

They carry a weightless load of dissolving associations –
A scented fug on an autumn day in the Orient Express;
And the persevering Trans-Siberian scattering scarlet
    sparks
Into the eyeless Mongol dark; and the locomotive bell
Clanging its lonely threat as someone took the prairie
    way
To the punishment of banishment, along the Atchison-
    Topeka line to Santa Fé.

William Plomer

*Steam trains have gone. It would be nice to believe that
this poem by the Poet Laureate was prophetic, but I fear
it is only wishful thinking.*

DILTON MARSH HALT

Was it worth keeping the Halt open,
    We thought as we looked at the sky
Red through the spread of the cedar-tree,
    With the evening train gone by ?

Yes, we said, for in summer the anglers use it,
    Two and sometimes three
Will bring their catches of rods and poles and perches
    To Westbury, home to tea.

There isn't a porter. The platform is made of sleepers.
    The guard of the last up-train puts out the light
And high over lorries and cattle the Halt unwinking
    Waits through the Wiltshire night.

O housewife safe in the comprehensive churning
   Of the Warminster launderette!
O husband down at the depot with car in car-park!
   The Halt is waiting yet.

And when all the horrible roads are finally done for,
   And there's no more petrol left in the world to burn,
Here to the Halt from Salisbury and from Bristol
   Steam trains will return.

Sir John Betjeman

*The flanged wheel has nearly come full circle. At the end
of the nineteenth century William Morris wrote down his
vision of how England might become perfect by the
twenty-first century. He describes a trip by rowing boat
from Hammersmith to Kelmscott. Certain landmarks are
missing.*

The railway having disappeared, and therewith the
various level bridges over the streams of Thames, we
were soon through Medley Lock and in the wide water
that washes Port Meadow, with its numerous population of geese nowise diminished; and I thought with
interest how its name and use had survived from the
older imperfect communal period, through the time of
the confused struggle and tyranny of the rights of
property, into the present rest and happiness of complete Communism.

William Morris, News from Nowhere, 1890

*But that is not quite the end of the story. Nor is this
delightful prayer.*

Forgive each wheel its gesture of repulsion;
And hope that I may sometime find direction;
That we may live at last under a quiet sun
Where no trains but God's sure thoughts need run.

Sidney Keyes, from For M. C., Written in the Train

The last word – a happy and optimistic one – goes to Agatha Christie. This dialogue seems to me perfect. Had she put 'God is the engine-driver', she might have been accused of writing pretentious cant. By making Poirot speak of le bon Dieu, *she avoids the pitfall and conveys her meaning triumphantly.*

From far behind them there came a long-drawn-out scream of an engine's whistle.

'That is that damned Blue Train,' said Lenox. 'Trains are relentless things, aren't they, Monsieur Poirot ? People are murdered and die, but they go on just the same. I am talking nonsense, but you know what I mean.'

'Yes, yes, I know. Life is like a train, Mademoiselle. It goes on. And it is a good thing that that is so.'

'Why ?'

'Because the train gets to its journey's end at last, and there is a proverb about that in your language, Mademoiselle.'

' "Journeys end in lovers meeting".' Lenox laughed. 'That is not going to be true for me.'

'Yes – yes, it is true. You are young, younger than you yourself know. Trust the train, Mademoiselle, for it is *le bon Dieu* who drives it.'

The whistle of the engine came again.

'Trust the train, Mademoiselle,' murmured Poirot again. 'And trust Hercule Poirot – *He knows*.'

Agatha Christie, *The Mystery of the Blue Train*, 1928

Acknowledgements

I cannot thank warmly enough Mari Prichard and Humphrey Carpenter without whose advice and support, not to mention admonishments, this anthology might never have been completed. My gratitude also goes to Jeremy Lewis for encouragement, Judith Chamberlain for patience, and Paul Surman for dreams.

The editor and publishers gratefully acknowledge permission to use copyright material in this book:

Dannie Abse: 'The Shunters' from *Collected Poems* (Hutchinson, 1977) © Dannie Abse 1970. Reprinted by permission of Anthony Sheil Assoc. Ltd.

W. H. Auden: 'Gare du Midi'. Copyright 1940 and renewed 1968 by W. H. Auden, from *Collected Poems* (ed. Mendelson). Extract from *The Orators: An English Study*. Both reprinted by permission of Faber & Faber Ltd., and Random House, Inc.

W. H. Auden and Christopher Isherwood: From *The Ascent of F6*. Reprinted by permission of Faber & Faber Ltd., and Curtis Brown Ltd., London.

Revd. W. Awdry: From *Oliver the Western Engine*. ©1969 Kaye & Ward Ltd. Reprinted by permission of the publisher.

Max Beerbohm: From *Zuleika Dobson*. Copyright 1911 by Dodd, Mead & Company, Inc. Copyright renewed 1938 by Max Beerbohm. Reprinted by permission of Wm. Heinemann Ltd., & Dodd, Mead & Company, Inc.

Hilaire Belloc: From *The Path to Rome* (Nelson, 1902). Reprinted by permission of A. D. Peters & Co. Ltd.

John Betjeman: 'Dilton Marsh Halt' and extract from 'Distant View of a Provincial Town', from *Collected Poems*. Reprinted by permission of John Murray (Publ.) Ltd.

John Buchan: From *The Thirty-nine Steps*. Reprinted by permission of A. P. Watt Ltd., for Lord Tweedsmuir and William Blackwood & Sons Ltd.

Humphrey Carpenter: From *J. R. R. Tolkien: A Biography*. Copyright © 1977 by George Allen & Unwin (Publ.) Ltd. Reprinted by permission of Allen & Unwin., and Houghton Mifflin Co.

G. K. Chesterton: 'The Fat White Woman Speaks' from *New Poems*; 'The Prehistoric Railway Station' from *Tremendous Trifles*. Reprinted by permission of A. P. Watt Ltd., for the Estate of G. K. Chesterton.

ACKNOWLEDGEMENTS

Agatha Christie: From *The Mystery of the Blue Train*. Copyright 1928 by Dodd, Mead & Company, Inc. Copyright renewed 1955 by Agatha Christie Mallowan. Reprinted by permission of Hughes Massie Ltd. & Dodd, Mead & Company, Inc.

Cyril Connolly ('Palinurus'): From *The Unquiet Grave* (Hamish Hamilton, 1945). Reprinted by permission of Deborah Rogers Ltd.

Frances Cornford: 'Figures on the Platform' and 'To a Fat Lady Seen from the Train', both from *Collected Poems* (Cresset, 1954). Reprinted by permission of the Hutchinson Publishing Group.

W. H. Davies: From *The Autobiography of a Super-Tramp*. Reprinted by permission of Jonahan Cape Ltd., for the Executors of the W. H. Davies Estate.

Lawrence Durrell: From *Justine*. Copyright © 1957 by Lawrence Durrell. Reprinted by permission of Faber & Faber Ltd., & E. P. Dutton. 'Vega' and 'Night Express' from *Collected Poems*. Copyright © 1960, 1972 by Lawrence Durrell. Reprinted by permission of Faber & Faber Ltd. and Viking Penguin, Inc. Extract from *A Smile in the Mind's Eye*. © Lawrence Durrell 1980. Reprinted by permission of Wildwood House Ltd., London, and Curtis Brown Ltd.

Clifford Dyment: From *The Railway Game* (1962). Reprinted by permission of J. M. Dent & Sons Ltd.

Patrick Leigh Fermor: From *Roumeli*. Reprinted by permission of John Murray (Publ.) Ltd.

F. Scott Fitzgerald: From *The Great Gatsby* and *Tender is the Night* (from The Bodley Head Scott Fitzgerald). Reprinted by permission of the publisher.

Ian Fleming: From *Live and Let Die* (Copyright 1954 by Glidrose Productions Ltd.) and *From Russia with Love* (© Glidrose Productions Ltd.) Reprinted by permission of Jonathan Cape Ltd., for Glidrose Productions, and Macmillan Publishing Co. Inc., New York.

E. M. Forster: From *Howards End* (1910). Reprinted by permission of King's College, Cambridge and The Society of Authors as the literary representative of the Estate of E. M. Forster.

Robert Frost: 'The Figure in the Doorway' from *The Poetry of Robert Frost*, edited by Edward Connery Lathem. Reprinted by permission of Jonathan Cape Ltd., for the Estate of Robert Frost.

John Fuller: 'In a Railway Compartment' from *Fairground Music*. Reprinted by permission of the author.

Robert Graves: 'The Next Time' from *Collected Poems* (Cassell,

1975). Reprinted by permission of A. P. Watt Ltd. for the author.

Graham Greene: From *The Human Factor* (Bodley Head/Simon & Schuster). Reprinted by permission of Laurence Pollinger Ltd., and Simon & Schuster, Inc.

Aldous Huxley: From *Crome Yellow* (pp. 7–8, 8–9). Copyright 1922 by Aldous Huxley. Reprinted by permission of Mrs Laura Huxley, Chatto & Windus Ltd., and Harper & Row, Publishers Inc.

Randall Jarrell: Extract from 'The Orient Express' from *The Complete Poems*. Copyright 1950 *The Nation*. Copyright renewed 1977 by Mrs Randall Jarrell. Reprinted by permission of Faber & Faber Ltd., and Farrar, Straus & Giroux, Inc.

Sidney Keyes: Extract from 'For M. C., Written in the Train' from *Collected Poems* (1945). Reprinted by permission of Routledge & Kegan Paul Ltd.

Rudyard Kipling: From *Kim*. Reprinted by permission of A. P. Watt Ltd., for the National Trust and Macmillan, London, Ltd.

E. V. Knox: 'The Everlasting Percy' from *Poems of Impudence*. Reprinted by permission of Ernest Benn.

Philip Larkin: 'One Man Walking a Deserted Platform' from *The North Ship*. Reprinted by permission of Faber & Faber Ltd.

Louis MacNeice: From *The Strings Are False* (Faber, 1965). Reprinted by permission of David Higham Assoc. Ltd.

Henry Miller: From *Letter to Anais Nin*, ed. & with an introduction by Gunther Stuhlman. Reprinted by permission of Peter Owen Ltd., London.

David Nobbs: From *The Death of Reginald Perrin*. Copyright 1975 David Nobbs. Reprinted by permission of Victor Gollancz Ltd., and Jonathan Clowes Ltd.

Flann O'Brien: From *The Best of Myles* (1968). Reprinted by permission of Granada Publishing Ltd., and A. M. Heath Ltd. for the Estate of the late Flann O'Brien.

Bruce Page: From *Philby, the Spy Who Betrayed a Generation* (1968). Reprinted by permission of André Deutsch Ltd.

William Plomer: 'The Last Train' from *Taste and Remember*. Reprinted by permission of Jonathan Cape Ltd., for the Estate of William Plomer.

W. R. Rodgers: 'The Train' from *Europa and the Bull* (1952). Reprinted by permission of Martin Secker & Warburg Ltd.

A. L. Rowse: 'Oxford Station' from *The Road to Oxford*. Reprinted by permission of Jonathan Cape Ltd.

Siegfried Sassoon: From *Memoirs of a Fox-Hunting Man*. Reprinted by permission of Faber & Faber Ltd., and K. S. Giniger Co. Inc., New York.

Robert Service: 'The Disaster' from *Songs For My Supper*, in *More Collected Verse of Robert Service*. Copyright 1953 by Dodd,

ACKNOWLEDGEMENTS

Mead & Company, Inc. 'Continental Trains' from *Selections From Unpublished Verse*, in *Later Collected Verse By Robert Service*. Copyright © 1954, 1956, 1965 by Dodd, Mead & Company, Inc. Copyright © 1960 by Germaine Service. Reprinted by permission of Ernest Benn, Dodd, Mead & Company Inc., and McGraw-Hill Ryerson, Canada.

Osbert Sitwell: From *Penny Foolish*, *By Train* (Macmillan). Reprinted by permission of David Higham Assoc. Ltd.

Stephen Spender: 'The Express'. Copyright 1934 and renewed 1962 by Stephen Spender, from *Collected Poems 1928–1953*. Reprinted by permission of Faber & Faber Ltd., and Random House, Inc.

Paul Theroux: From *The Great Railway Bazaar* (Hamish Hamilton, 1975) and from *The Family Arsenal* (Hamish Hamilton, 1976). Reprinted by permission of Gillon Aitken for the author.

Dylan Thomas: From *Adventures in the Skin Trade* (Dent). Reprinted by permission of David Higham Assoc. Ltd.

Anthony Thwaite: 'Sunday Afternoons' from *The Owl in the Tree*. © OUP 1963. Reprinted by permission of Oxford University Press.

John Wain: From *The Smaller Sky* (Macmillan, 1967). Reprinted by permission of Curtis Brown Ltd., London.

P. G. Wodehouse: From *Meet Mr. Mulliner* and *Uncle Fred in the Springtime*. Reprinted by permission of A. P. Watt Ltd., for the Estate of P. G. Wodehouse and Hutchinson Publishing Group Ltd.

While every effort has been made to secure permission we may have failed in a few cases to trace the copyright holder. We apologize for any apparent negligence.

The illustrations in this book were taken from the following sources: *Fann Street Letter Foundry*, *A General Specimen* (London, 1873); W. J. Gordon, *Every-Day Life on the Railroad* (London, n.d.); *Miller & Richard's Typefounders Catalogue* (Edinburgh, 1873); John Pendleton, *Our Railways* Volumes I and II (London, 1894); *The Train* Volume I (London, 1856); Frederick S. Williams, *Our Iron Roads* (London, 1852).

Index

Abse, Dannie, 24, 39–40
Arnold, Matthew, 67–8
Ashley, Kenneth, 96–7
Auden, W. H., 32, 72, 95
Awdry, W., 91–2

Beerbohm, Max, 41, 80–1
Belloc, Hilaire, 65
Bennett, Arnold, 48–9, 69–70, 81
Betjeman, John, 65, 104–5
British Rail, 99
Brooke, Rupert, 36
Browning, Robert, 63
Buchan, John, 50

Carpenter, Humphrey, 95
Carroll, Lewis, 93–4
Causley, Charles, 19–20
Chesterton, G. K., 9–10, 56
Chetwynd, Tom, 75–6
Christie, Agatha, 56, 106
Cobb, Richard, 66
Coleridge, Mary, 17
Connolly, Cyril, *see* Palinurus
Cornford, Frances, 56, 102
Crane, Hart, 86

Davidson, John, 19, 29–30, 53
Davies, W. H., 84–5
Dickens, Charles, 1–2, 14–15, 43, 53–4, 79, 99–100
Dickinson, Emily, 16–17
Dodgson, Charles, *see* Carroll, Lewis
Durrell, Lawrence, 23–4, 36–7, 60–1
Dyment, Clifford, 79

Eliot, T. S., 67
Elliott, Ebenezer, 5–6
Emerson, R. W., 10–11

Fermor, Patrick Leigh, 94
Fitzgerald, F. Scott, 53, 59
Fleming, Ian, 24–5, 95–6
Forster, E. M., 32–3
Fowler, W. Warde, 97–8
Frost, Robert, 55
Fuller, John, 93

Gillinan, S. W., 47–8
Grahame, Kenneth, 69, 90–1
Graves, Robert, 40–1
Gray, Thomas, 66–7
Green, Roger, 88
Greene, Graham, 63, 76–7
Guardian, 68–9, 73
Gulliver, Richard, 98

Hardy, Thomas, 86–7
Hawthorne, Nathaniel, 12
Hobson, Harold, 101–2
Huxley, Aldous, 49–50, 64–5

Isherwood, Christopher, 72

Jarrell, Randall, 57
Jefferies, Richard, 77–8

Keats, John, 67
Keyes, Sidney, 105
Kilvert, Francis, 20–1
Kipling, Rudyard, 16, 21, 37
Knightley, Philip, 77
Knox, E. V., 89–90

Larkin, Philip, 71
Lawrence, D. H., 87–8
Leitch, David, 77

MacNeice, Louis, 66, 96
Mansfield, Katherine, 23
Masefield, John, 89
Melville, Herman, 42
Miller, Henry, 63–4

Monro, Harold, 57, 71
Morris, William, 105

Nesbit, E., 37–8, 50–1
Nobbs, David, 74

O'Brien, Flann, 51–2
Owen, Wilfred, 82–3

Page, Bruce, 77
Palinurus (Cyril Connolly), 27–8
Peacock, T. L., 7–8, 20
Plomer, William, 103–4
Pope, Alexander, 66

Rodgers, W. R., 58–9
Rowse, A. L., 41–2
Ruskin, John, 8–9
Rutter, Owen, 83–4

Sassoon, Siegfried, 49
Selver, Paul, 70
Service, Robert, 25–6, 100–1

Sitwell, Osbert, 21
Smith, Sydney, 6
Spender, Stephen, 21–2
Stephen, J. K., 4–5
Stevenson, R. L., 12–13, 54–5
Surtees, R. S., 18–19

Theroux, Paul, 57–8, 74–5
Thomas, Dylan, 30
Thomas, Edward, 39
Thoreau, H. D., 11, 44
Thwaite, Anthony, 30–1
Tolkien, J. R. R., 95
Trollope, Anthony, 29, 61–2, 81–2

Upward, Edward, 94

Wain, John, 31–2
White, E. B., 67
Whittier, J. G., 45
Wilde, Oscar, 34–5, 87
Wodehouse, P. G., 34, 81
Wood, Charles, 101
Wordsworth, William, 3–4